CAMPUS U.S.A.

CAMPUS
U. S. A.

Portraits of American Colleges in Action

D A V I D   B O R O F F

Harper & Brothers, Publishers, New York

CAMPUS U.S.A.

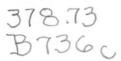

To JOHN FISCHER, *Editor of* HARPER'S *Magazine,*
who made this book possible

CONTENTS

INTRODUCTION:
What the Catalogues Never Tell You

There is an old bromide that a student can get a good college education anywhere—if only he is earnest enough. This is true, but only if one defines college education narrowly as a body of knowledge and a vocational skill like accounting or animal husbandry. If, however, the student sets his sights on a rich, full personal development—as well as knowledge—then it matters very much where he goes to college. In fact, it matters his whole lifetime.

During the last decade or so, educators have become persuaded of some fairly obvious things which, surprisingly, eluded them earlier. Their main discovery is that each college or university has a personality. Anybody who has spent time at a college knows it, feels it, but can't always define it. Even the Ivy League schools, so formidably monolithic to the outsider, show dramatic differences. Just try confusing a Yale student with one from Harvard!

Some schools are friendly, others are cold. In some, the intellectual life flourishes; in others the intellectual has to fight for his existence. There are fraternity schools and bohemian schools, rural and urban, religious and militantly secular. And there are those colleges—more interesting than most—in which many of these tendencies are complexly intertwined, and the student must define himself as he unravels the twisted strands.

The institutional personality may not be identical with the official philosophy of a college; it may even run counter to it. But it's what counts. And it counts because each generation of college students transmits it to the next. It's *their* culture—not the professors'—and unconsciously they protect it as jealously as any group protects its heritage.

Another arresting fact: Students not only assimilate the institutional culture—it stamps them for life. Those paltry years from seventeen or eighteen to twenty-one or twenty-two shape them as few future events will. The choice of college is as crucial as the choice of mate or job. It's not upper-class fatuity that makes one middle-aged person say of another significantly, "He went to Princeton," or "She went to Bryn Mawr." There is a recognition that this was their training ground—and the training is for keeps. The term "finishing school," applied to certain two-year colleges, is as accurate as its implied snobbery is absurd.

So it's a very important matter what college a young person attends—and not merely in terms of the cash value of a particular degree, or the equally vulgar matter of the "contacts" one can make. At stake are all the subtle dimensions that constitute a human being. How a mature man or woman will respond to a painting, or a piece of music, or another human being, what books he reads—or more to the point, *whether* he reads—all of these are molded by those four fleeting years. Even his capacity for independent thinking is created, or at least the foundation is laid, during that period. Critical thinking cannot really be taught; there is no formula for it. But the habit is something a student absorbs in an intellectual atmosphere at once bold and supportive.

All of this is well known these days. The field of educational sociology, which measures students this way and that, is in an unparalleled boom. But sociologists, though they have taught us a great deal, cannot evoke the vibrant reality of a particular college. For one thing, they anatomize and isolate. What we need is the organic reality, the way it really is.

This is a job, you might say, for the literary artist. In truth, novelists have come closer to rendering the college scene than social scientists. But novelists, too, have failed. The melancholy truth is that in almost all academic novels—Mary McCarthy's *Groves of Academe* or Stringfellow Barr's *Strictly Academic,* for example—the surgical steel has been applied *only* to faculty and administration. The students are fobbed off as lovable barbarians or monsters of precocity. (The reason is not hard to locate:

people write academic novels because of intellectual vendettas or because they have scores to settle with those in power. Why bother with students?)

Nor do colleges show any aptitude for describing themselves. In the long historical run, our own time may well be described as the Age of Public Relations. No self-respecting college today is without its News Service or Information Office, or whatever other euphemism it employs to conceal the naked stridency of publicity. The upshot of this is a nervous circumspection that makes all colleges, from the lowly ones, snuggled in obscure valleys, to the arrogant giants, sound remarkably the same. And even when they spell out the minutiae of their programs they obscure as much as they reveal.

Take social life, for example. Should the facts about campus social life have to be gleaned through an underground of gossip and warmed-over anecdote? Isn't such information vital to college students, for whom the campus, despite all our pious breast-beating, remains marriage mart as well as classroom? One need only have the faintest empathy for college students to know how much anxiety and intensity are invested in their social lives.

It is not enough for college catalogues and brochures to reveal that there are fraternities and sororities on campus. What the student really wants to know is: How essential is it that he affiliate? Will he be lonely, and badgeless, and excluded if he doesn't join? And other vital things remain undisclosed by official publications. What are campus attitudes towards dress? towards study? towards sexual behavior? What are the prevailing models, so to speak, of masculinity and femininity on campus? Is the school a play school? And if it is, are there countercurrents, or will the serious student have to spend his energies sloughing off the trivial and the irrelevant? What ideas are fashionable on campus? What interest groups are there? What are the outlets—other than frivolous water fights and fraternity hazing—for the release of the dissident, aggressive energies of adolescence?

There are striking disparities between the official images, the canned institutional propaganda as presented in catalogues, and the reality within. The Harvard catalogue is a bloated volume of 1,118 pages of closely packed print, but nowhere is Harvard's personality defined. Those in the know talk of the tone of the place—a redoubtable blend of self-confidence and self-effacement, keen curiosity and sophisticated restraint. But the catalogue never tells you. There is a short paragraph devoted to the tutorials, but the austere prose hardly hints at the intellectual carnage that takes place. And nothing in the Radcliffe catalogue tells you why the school magnetizes bright girls everywhere. It is not only the school's rousingly high standards but the fact that there are all those thousands of males to draw from—graduate students too! The Radcliffe girl need not worry about junior year slump—the specter that haunts college girls everywhere who outgrow, or exhaust, the local undergraduates.

The Sarah Lawrence catalogue preeningly announces: "In a small discussion group, all students have an opportunity to participate and to bring to the group the results of their own thinking and reading." All well and good. The catalogue conjures up an image of intimacy, of professor and student joined in a common intellectual enterprise. What it fails to point out is that the very intimacy can be defeating. The atmosphere is so warm and loving and familial that it becomes an act of filial impiety for a student to challenge her teacher.

Birmingham–Southern College states neutrally in its catalogue: "The Cellar, a student meeting place in the basement of the library, is open daily from 9 A.M. to 12 noon." What it doesn't say is that the Cellar, once characterized as the school's "existentialist bistro," is the nerve center of the dissenters and outsiders who dare criticize Southern orthodoxy. And students at Birmingham–Southern define their own ethos in their relationship to the Cellar, ranging from those for whom it is a spiritual haven, to the well-brought-up Southern miss who said flutteringly, "Why, I wouldn't dare go in there!"

The purpose of this book, then, is to describe, intimately and searchingly, colleges of various types. Included are state universities, a municipal college, church-related colleges, progressive schools, women's colleges, and a big Ivy League institution. All areas of the country are represented, and there are big city colleges, small-town and rural ones. The book encompasses nearly the entire spectrum of higher education in America.

Prospective college students, their parents, or the many thousands already in college who are contemplating transfer (damning evidence of bad choosing) may profit from this book. It should help them answer the key questions: Where do I belong? Where will I be happy? Which college will bring about the greatest growth?

But I am not implying that the trick is simply to match the college and the student—a dull, gray, compatible marriage. There is a lot to be said for conflict, polarity, opposition. Out of rugged encounter comes intellectual and moral muscle. A certain kind of rural boy or girl may well profit from a sophisticated urban school. (With this in mind, New York University now offers a junior year in New York City—an admirable idea.) And a New York City provincial can achieve undreamed of breakthroughs by living in a small town or rural school. A certain kind of youngster needs a stable, homogeneous setting—a kind of academic Big Daddy; others, who are more venturesome, thrive in an atmosphere where choices have to be made between one life style and another.

College guidance is an art—an almost impossible art—based on incredibly complex imponderables. But it can make sense only when one knows what colleges are *really* like.

This book is intended to contribute to that end.

Colleges with a National Clientele

IMPERIAL HARVARD

All roads lead to Harvard Square. The visitor to Cambridge has an immediate sense of being engulfed by the university. A curious spatial distortion sets in after a few days: Boston, just over the river and a few minutes away, seems miles distant. You walk along the Charles River, and as far as the eye can see there are the towers of Harvard.

There is a quiet sobriety about Cambridge, and the town is little given to boosterism. Nevertheless there is a calm expectation that the great and the mighty will ultimately debark here. The proprietor of the modest rooming house at which I spent a night had copies of *Scientific American* on his table and at two in the morning engaged me in a discussion about Kierkegaard.

It is this quality of isolation, coupled with intensity, that impelled a Harvard professor to describe the place as "The Magic Mountain." Yet, like a dagger aimed at its throat, there is a street running in among Harvard's buildings, lined with seedy bars frequented by the local Visigoths. They are full of sullen resentments for the Harvard patricians. There is a town-and-gown situation in Cambridge, and the police cars are always ready.

Harvard is casual about its greatness. There is an apocryphal story about the occasion when President Lowell of Harvard visited President Taft at the White House. A man who enquired about Lowell's whereabouts was told, "*President* Lowell is in Washington visiting *Mr.* Taft." A recent anecdote illustrates the same theme. A Harvard-bound freshman in the Midwest reverently packed his clarinet and chamber-music scores for the long trip east. He had been playing in a wood-wind group at home. "Where will you find an oboe or bassoon player?" he was asked. "But I'm going to Harvard!" he answered with exasperation.

3

Harvard has a diversity, along with its scrupulous sense of privacy, which neither a counseling service nor the big-brotherly ministrations of the "house" system can subvert. "You can be schizoid at Harvard, and nobody would know it," a student observed. But at the same time it has a stubborn sense of identity. There may not be an archetypal Harvard man, but unquestionably there are Harvard men.

Early in my visit I confronted the awesome reality of this Harvard mystique. The university has about it a sense of New England rectitude and bleak modesty. The president's office is unrelievedly severe. President Pusey sits at a small, old, handsomely polished table, the kind you can buy in any Connecticut antique shop. Harvard seems spare, dry, cautious, and angular. Decorum is tight and mandatory. There is a side of Harvard which is Proper Bostonian, and there is a sense in which everyone is irredeemably "square."

And when Harvard is not being restrained and correct, it is ironic—as if it had a sense of the absurdity of some of its own postures. The irony also issues from an invulnerable sense of security. We can afford to poke fun at ourselves, it says. It is stimulated, too, by a peculiar double vision. Harvard is at once the oldest of American colleges—well over three hundred years—and the most contemporary. Though it is a locus of power in an age when universities are becoming huge bureaucracies, it has a vivid sense of the past.

There is little panoply of rank at Harvard. Everyone from President Pusey to the most submerged tutor is addressed by the sobersided "Mister." This is not to say that there aren't hierarchies and a furious scramble for status.

With tightly reined modesty, Harvard men take its superiority for granted. Highly varied in their viewpoints, students and faculty are united on one article of faith: the greatness of the Harvard idea. It expresses itself in the mindless elegance of the "Clubbies," in the slashing iconoclasm of the student newspaper editors, in the zeal of the straight A students prowling the stacks of Widener Library. Even the Beat Generation representatives base their disdain for Harvard's sterilities on an assumption of the university's superiority.

It is easy to marshal evidence for Harvard's excellence. Ninety per cent of those who enter receive their degrees (the national average is under 50 per cent). About half of all Harvard students are candidates for honors in their fields. The faculty is full of the glamor boys of the academic world—people like poet Archibald MacLeish, Harry Levin in literature, Paul Tillich in theology, Arthur Schlesinger, Jr., and Crane Brinton in history. Worthy of note, too, is its salary scale, the best in the country. (The average salary of a full professor is $16,000 a year.) On the other hand, the pressure to produce—publish or perish—is as cruel at Harvard as anywhere. And part of Harvard's greatness certainly is its remarkable library resources—6.5 million items in eighty-eight separate libraries.

Harvard's greatness is not confined to its campus. Her graduates occupy seats of power everywhere—most conspicuously at the moment in Washington, where President Kennedy, himself a member of the class of 1940, staffed seventeen top-ranking posts in his administration with Harvard alumni and faculty. (Faculty depredations included the talented Dean McGeorge Bundy.) One of the current jokes about the new Harvard-on-the-Potomac is that office coffee breaks have been banned—replaced by class reunions.

But only the sternest national requirements can pry Harvard faculty from their Cambridge haven. At a time when professors everywhere are madly peripatetic, engaged in campus-and-continent-hopping on multitudinous grants, one Harvard officer asked quietly, "Who would want to leave Harvard?"

Appreciation for the idiosyncratic is part of the Harvard mystique. Cantabrigians take pride in the offbeat and odd. "When you're eccentric *and* Groton," an alumnus pointed out, "then you're very eccentric." Part of this is an aristocratic tolerance of the deviant. Part of it is the warping of personality that has always been a feature of the harsh emotional and physical climate of New England. And it goes without saying that the idiosyncratic must never get too far out of hand.

The mystique also means an acceptance of Harvard rituals and private humor. It means good manners, unobtrusive and graceful, sherry in the rooms, and jokes about local landmarks like the

Russian bells in the tower of Lowell House. ("We can't all have Russian bells," a tutor in another house said, with mock bitterness.) It means also urbane, scornful condescension toward Yale, a good-natured contempt for Dartmouth ("brutes who come with snow on their boots"), and a reluctance even to discuss Princeton, with its snobbish barbarities.

The Harvard mystique has its roots, too, in a past of incomparable brilliance. Santayana and William James, Longfellow and James Russell Lowell, the long line of writers from Thoreau and Emerson to T. S. Eliot and Wallace Stevens—these giants still haunt the campus. And undergraduates will calmly show you where F.D.R. roomed, and will suggest that it was his failure to make the club of his choice that redirected his energies into politics.

There are 4,500 undergraduates at Harvard and 1,150 Radcliffe girls. (Harvard is increasingly coeducational, as they will tell you, "in practice though not in theory.") There is also a large graduate school of arts and sciences, with some 1,700 students. (About 500 Harvard undergraduates are registered for graduate courses.) Because academic luminaries abound, the faculty is reputed to be interested primarily in graduate courses. Trying to counter this tendency, the university has them teach undergraduate courses, assigning them to houses and involving them in tutorials.

Harvard College is free from vocationalism. "We don't have undergraduate business courses," President Pusey told me. "I suppose you might say we're snobbish about that." On the other hand, Harvard's Graduate School of Business confers more degrees, largely M.B.A.'s, than any of its other graduate schools. About 60 to 70 per cent of the college's graduates go on to advanced study—an imposing number.

Harvard is not a rich man's school. "The Boston blue bloods set the pattern," President Pusey remarked, "but now we're broadly representative of the whole country." It is aristrocratic but in the Jeffersonian sense; it pursues the ideal of an intellectual elite regardless of class or social origin. Almost two thousand students receive some kind of financial assistance—scholarships, loans, or job aid. On the other hand, slightly more than half of last year's freshmen came from private schools, and a Harvard administrator has observed that if the standards of public high schools continue to decline, that proportion will increase.

There are, of course, many scions of wealthy families at Harvard. Former President Conant is supposed to have remarked, with Yankee sagacity, that if young people are going to inherit great influence, you might as well get your hands on them.

Harvard is a resident college, but about four hundred students commute. They are organized into a nonresident house where they have lunch and carry on an almost normal range of extra-curricular activities. The commuters constitute a minority within the college, and they are variously stereotyped as poor Irish or Jews, and likely to be grinds. There are, however, amusing discordancies in these images. Thirty-eight per cent of the commuting students attended private secondary schools, and last year there were three accidents involving commuters driving Jaguars.

Students choose courses for "distribution" (General Education) and "concentration" (major). Harvard has long since dropped President Eliot's free-elective system, which enormously expanded the horizons of education, but was susceptible to abuse by those—emulating Mario in Santayana's *The Last Puritan*—who studied whimsically unrelated subjects. General Education, in which (with an assist from Columbia) Harvard pioneered, now ensures some contact with the broad cultural tradition of the Western world. Each student is required to take three General Education courses during his first two years, one in each of the major areas of knowledge—the humanities, the natural sciences, and the social sciences. The guiding principle, at the risk of producing intellectual dandies, is "to take a limited amount of subject matter and show how a discipline works."

For a college with an undiminished ardor about the past, Harvard is in one respect flamboyantly up to date. Its courses have such modish-sounding titles as "Crisis and the Individual" and "Uses of the Comic Spirit." The "Gen Ed" courses, as they are called, are discursive and wide-roaming, in that new pattern of American higher education which despairs to cover everything, since knowledge is so huge, and contents itself with sampling.

Thus a year's humanities course might sprint through the centuries from *The Iliad* to *War and Peace*.

Literature is taught "less to disseminate knowledge" than as "a meaningful commentary upon life." Social Science I mediates between old-fashioned fact swallowing ("a backbone of straightforward historical chronology") and imaginative intellectual exploration ("to find, if not a philosophy, at least a pattern in history").

One of the pivotal features of the Harvard program is the tutorial, adapted from the Oxford-Cambridge pattern. The Harvard student carries only four courses at a time, as against five in most schools, and in his sophomore year he is assigned a tutor in his field of concentration. He reads under the latter's direction, prepares papers for him, and periodically meets with him for a session of remorseless intellectual exchange.

I heard a tape recording of a tutor and tutee locked in cerebral combat as they discussed *Huckleberry Finn*. What was striking about it was that the tutee clearly outpointed the tutor. It was an astonishing performance—the student, avid, unabashedly precocious, a virtuoso of the quick formulation and the dazzling epigram; the tutor, gifted and articulate, but overpowered. On the other hand, I listened to a tape recording of a soft-voiced Radcliffe girl, helpless before the intellectual onslaught of her tutor.

The tutor also serves as an adviser. (During his first year, the student has a special freshman adviser.) Here Harvard has made an interesting attempt to reconcile its traditional arrangements with the new administrative technology. In many colleges there is an enormous boom of guidance departments, counseling apparatus, and administrative deans. Students are thought of as "student personnel" and there are departments of Personnel Service—which makes a college sound vaguely like a plastics factory. A professor friend of mine reported with dismay the cancerous growth of administration at his college—classroom after classroom, then corridor after corridor, swallowed up by administration.

There is, to be sure, a traditional hostility between the man of ideas and the technician who manipulates people. But at Harvard almost all counseling and administration is decentralized, handled by faculty members of the student's house. Thus there is no serious split between teachers and administrators. Harvard may have as much administrative machinery as any other college, but it is far less obtrusive.

"The curious thing about this place," former Dean McGeorge Bundy pointed out, "is the way the atmosphere conditions the institutional arrangements. Our tradition of autonomy runs counter to a top-heavy administrative setup."

What can one say about the composite personality of the Harvard student? There is, of course, an old tradition of the "gentleman's C." To the *echt* Harvard man of yore, a gentleman should schedule no course before 11 A.M. or in a classroom above the second floor. And there is the folklore of the gilded youth whose orbit ranged through parties, clubs, and weekends. He put a suitcase in the middle of his room and turned up occasionally for a fresh shirt.

Alas, for the graces of a lost world! The intellectual languor that Henry Adams noted ("no one took Harvard College seriously") is irretrievably gone. Today there is intense intellectuality; if anything, it cuts too wide a swath. To be sure, no voice from the past is wholly lost. Intellectual zealotry is mitigated by the older tradition of urbane negligence. It is still possible at Harvard to have bad grades and yet consider yourself well educated.

Grades are deprecated, but intellectual rivalry is fierce. One instructor described it as "lateral competition." Students measure their intellectual attainments against each other. Even more anxiety is produced by the tendency to appraise one's performance against the vast backdrop of the Harvard past.

"If you put out less than your best," a student said ruefully, "you feel that you're letting someone vaguely in the background down."

(Harvard eventually calls all its sons to an accounting at their twenty-fifth reunion, when each—like J. P. Marquand's H. M. Pulham, Esq.—is expected to summarize for the class report what he has accomplished in life.)

Undergraduates have a sense not of moving intellectually but of being hurtled. In their first year they find themselves doing long papers for which the short sprints of high school had not prepared them. ("Write a 2,000–3,000 word essay comparing the concepts of wisdom and justice held by the authors of the Book of Job, the Book of Ecclesiastes, and *Prometheus Bound*.")

Some take a beating from their first exams. "At Harvard," one of them remarked, "November is the cruelest month." They confront their heavy reading program with fear and trembling. Nor are they alone in their awe. Robert Frost, reviewing the reading load of a General Education course, exclaimed, "My God, that's more reading than I do in a year!"

Students and faculty talk about the "Exeter syndrome"—a term which applies to secondary-school graduates, especially from Exeter, who are overprepared for Harvard.

"At fifteen," a faculty member explained, "they are handling the verbal ingenuities of the Metaphysical Poets. They're living off intellectual capital they haven't fully earned."

Recently there have been experiments with freshmen seminars to counteract the feeling of some students that they have had the equivalent of a freshman experience at prep school. (Harvard pays a price for its own persuasiveness. Its General Education program has, in some measure, been introduced into the more ambitious secondary schools.)

Another familiar pathology is that of the "valedictorian's ego." The college swarms with top high school students who have had to divest themselves of their former grandeur.

"Even students who have no right to do so take ideas seriously," a professor remarked. Another, from a lower-middle-class background, observed with resolute fairness, "Part of the upper-class ethos is that intellectualism is good." Deference to the life of the mind is as much a part of the Harvard landscape as the ubiquitous chino pants, sports jacket, and narrow tie.

But the pursuit of ideas takes on the coloring of these chastened times. The poetry of thought is muted, exhilaration is damped down. There is a sense of energy tempered by coolness. "Nobody would say he's searching for the truth," a student said. "That would seem far too dramatic." They settle for the more moderate goal of being well educated. Nobody speculates wildly if he can help it. "The important thing is not to be wrong," a senior said. Another added: "There is a terrific fear of seeming naive."

Even in the unregimented student life of the Yard, there has been a certain failure of nerve, a hint of the youthful generation's prudence. All last spring the freshmen threatened a riot, which merely sputtered fitfully on a few occasions. Radcliffe girls, hearing of the possibility, sniffed scornfully.

"What sort of riot is it when it has to be planned?" one of them asked.

When students are exhorted to take the leap of action, by their professors who grew up in a more adventurous ethic, they are inclined to retort, "All right, your generation did. Look at the shape the world is in now." One of them remarked, "Nobody feels like going out with a billboard saying, 'Adam Smith Saves.'" The trend is toward synthesis, possibly encouraged by the eclectic and integrative character of the General Education courses. Zeal definitely is out of fashion. Barely seven hundred students belong to political organizations, and at a meeting concerned with nuclear policy, I saw only a forlorn handful.

Idealism also is suspect, though by no means absent. I sat with a group of Harvard seniors. One of them, an economics major, was planning graduate work in Far Eastern studies with a view to going into business in an underdeveloped part of the Orient. He was hesitant, however, to acknowledge any altruistic motive. His friends' prompting finally forced him to admit that, in a small way, he wanted to set up his own Point Four program.

Willam Alfred, a poet now teaching at Harvard, had attended Brooklyn College during the unbuttoned thirties and forties.

"Brooklyn College gave you an opportunity to be foolish," he recalled. "And that was healthy. When I came here, much more precision was demanded. Reading a text became a moral act. My task is to show students how much they really know. I have to break down their circumspection."

As one might expect, the more "inward" subjects—like literature and philosophy—have gained in popularity. Government has declined. An interest in history has been spurred by the impulse, common after a war, to take stock of the national experience.

How do the students respond to Harvard? The experience

tends to be more astringent than euphoric. "You don't enjoy Harvard the first two years, but you respect it," a student said grimly. Freshmen develop a tough, sinewy independence.

"You're forced to make your own decisions here," a student said. "You either grow up or you break."

There is no attendance check in most classes, deadlines for papers are flexible, and there are "reading periods" when classes are suspended to enable students to catch up.

There is a certain reciprocal politesse at Harvard. Students are treated like responsible adults, and usually they behave accordingly. Manners can degenerate into an empty formalism (which is the hostile stereotype many people have of Harvard), but there is really too much sparkle and intellectual animation for that to happen. What *can* happen is that mandatory politeness can result in less intimate communication.

Autonomy can also mean isolation for some students, despite the house pattern. Theoretically, the tutors assigned to the houses are supposed to make contact with students. In practice, they are caught up in their own affairs—graduate studies and tutorials—and in the dining room are more likely to sit around with a few choice students, or with other tutors, than to seek out the sad and the lonely. Yet contact with faculty is there for the asking—it has institutional support—and I saw students drop into tutors' rooms to borrow a book or just to chat.

There are seven houses designed to defeat Harvard's vastness and impersonality. Students who live in a house are required to have most of their meals there, which has tempered the hegemony of the clubs and has prevented fraternity inroads. (There is only one fraternity.) Each house has its own social life and activities, each develops its own rites. Lowell House, for example, has a "High Table Dinner," a black-tie affair to which precisely a dozen tutors, six guests, and six seniors are invited. After the dinner, they adjourn to the common room, with full punctilio, for coffee and cigars.

There is a certain ambivalence about the house pattern. On the one hand, there is a desire to foster a house personality; on the other, the crux of the "house plan" is heterogeneity. Thus if a house becomes swollen with muscle, it will bypass athletes in favor of intellectuals. Nevertheless each house has a kind of tenuous identity: Winthrop is athletic, Eliot is reputed to be full of "Clubbies" and "Preppies," Adams is vaguely bohemian, etc.

One of the most spirited of Harvard phenomena is the *Crimson*, the superbly turned out undergraduate newspaper. Independent of faculty control, the *Crimson* owns its own building and printing plant; and one can see bulky middle-aged pressmen in work clothes getting instructions from their apple-cheeked bosses. *Crimson* editors have a long tradition of iconoclasm, defiance of university administration, and a collegiate raffishness. A Radcliffe girl epitomized a nearly universal sentiment when she said, "I often feel irritated by their opinionatedness, but they're stimulating."

They tend to be liberal, anticlub, and passionately pro-Harvard. A few years ago, when a Jewish student was a candidate for election by his fellow-editors as president of the *Crimson*, his opponent made anti-Semitic pronouncements. One of the deans told the Jewish candidate, with some amusement, "You probably put him up to this." The *Crimson* ethos was such that a good Jewish candidate, beleaguered by prejudice, could win hands down. He did.

Cleveland Amory recently recalled the heady delights of being president of *Crimson:* "It was a job so exalted that though you believed that life afterwards would probably go on from there, nothing else, on earth at least, would really matter very much. You had done all there was to do."

One of the *Crimson's* gaudiest annual sports is issuing the "Confidential Guide to Freshman Courses," a bargain at fifty cents. Fine Arts 13 is whimsically described as "A ground-glass view of art from clay to Klee, given in a half-darkened cellar of Fogg on a bright white screen by dimly-visible men. A good though whirlwind introduction." Of an English instructor, the guide said bluntly: "Everybody agreed that his fall-term lectures were both intolerably dull and useless for the course."

A chemistry instructor inspired this vignette: "He had the amusing habit of revealing the bleached hair of Annexites Radcliffe by darkening the lecture room and shining a powerful fluorescent light toward them." A professor described as "dull" wrote a letter to *Crimson* asking plaintively, "What will my grandchildren think?"

Crimson executives meet with President Pusey regularly, but they come in the spirit of potentates conferring with another chief of state. They are minimally subject to the administration's control. If anything, the lines of power move quite the other way. The *Crimson*'s deadpan japeries are all in a spirit of fun, but the Boston papers report them, sometimes distortedly, and then the wire services pick them up. This sometimes gives rise to administrative disquiet. June is also a time of small dread for the president. "The *Crimson* boys fish about in the honorary degrees," he said. "They know our sensitive spots." In general, there is an admirable permissiveness.

"Students grow up in the *Crimson*," he added. "They have to make their mistakes. By and large, they do well with their responsibilities."

Two faces of the *Crimson* are reflected in recent pieces. One was an editorial about the Yale-Harvard game. In a spirit of Ivy League raillery, the newspaper declared:

On our part, we have always looked forward to the Yale game. It is refreshing to meet our clean-living Rivals Through The Centuries, and see how wonderfully they have progressed since we founded their Alma Mater a few centuries ago. They dress so nicely, and are so delightfully clean-shaven, and one always knows that they will be such wonderful financial successes in life. We like Yale—it's much milder.

In a spirit of high dudgeon, however, the *Crimson* excoriated Princeton for its unhappy club episode. John E. McNees depicted the nervous chatter, the tightly drawn anxieties of "bicker" day, when elections to the Princeton clubs are held. Then he went on to define the social pariah—locally known as a "wonk"—at bicker-time: "He wears outlandish ties, dirty sweaters, and baggy pants. Not only lacking a crew-cut, he is in bad need of a barber. . . . His idea of kicks is playing the violin. The girls he dates, when he dates at all, are dogs." With mordant irony, the writer observed that in the view of the Princeton clubs "this precisely describes the sort of man who must at all costs be kept out. It is also a fairly accurate portrait of Einstein. . . ."

The *Crimson*'s wrath against Princeton may well be a displacement of its own animus against Harvard's clubs. The parallels are uncomfortably tight. The Clubbies show the same relentless disapproval of the wonk. Some critics have charged the *Crimson* with an unseemly silence about Harvard's own princes of snobbery. The usual rejoinder is that the Clubbies constitute no more than 15 per cent of the college population.

Harvard officials, agreeably candid about almost everything else, maintained a well modulated silence about the clubs; it was the one area in which I got a run-around. But one sees the silent clubhouses, the sports cars, the lank elegance, and the Harris tweeds. The Clubbies make their presence felt out of all proportion to their meager numbers. Their counsels don't prevail, but they do have the effect of taking some first-rate people out of circulation.

A *Crimson* article not too long ago described the milieu of the clubs with judicious detachment. During "punching" (pledging) season, *Crimson* reported, "host members will be carefully on the lookout for the punchee's social grace, his dexterity with a fingerbowl, his conversational adroitness. . . . For the Club members, college becomes a highly limiting experience instead of the broadening one it might be."

There is, of course, a rationale for the clubs. Harvard, for all its intellectual hurly-burly, is a conservative institution with a deep respect for the past, which includes an aristocratic tradition. The clubs keep some sense of it alive (Harvard used to rank its students socially) and to some extent reduce the pressure toward other forms of social stratification, by providing those who wish it with an isolated and relatively innocent playground.

"Ironically," *Crimson* points out, "it is the most repellent qualities of the Clubs that give the system this advantage. Their snobbishness, their secrecy, their uncreativity, their preoccupation with an isolated social world all tend to dissuade most undergraduates from any wish to join."

Boy meets girl at Harvard in an atmosphere of stylized distaste.

The cold sneer directed at Radcliffe girls is a fixed part of the Harvard physiognomy. In the end, after the requisite sparring, they marry.

Harvard's comments on the local women are predictable. Radcliffe girls are too academic and "raise the curve"—that is, make courses harder by raising the average. A Radcliffe "jolly-up" is described as simply an "overcrowded mixer, full of sour cider, and girls primed with smart repartee."

The real grievance is that there aren't enough girls. Beneath the studied indifference there is a lively respect for the "Cliffies" pedaling to class on English bikes in their drab Brooks Brothers raincoats.

A recent *Harvard Alumni Bulletin* said piously: "One can only hope that when the millennium comes and the two noble institutions become one, they will let us call it Harvard rather than Radcliffe University."

The girls have the best of two worlds. They have their own identity as a woman's college, and they have Harvard's resources. "An administration without faculty," Radcliffe ships its students to class at Harvard, and the girls sit in a line like discreet little sparrows. Short-haired, for the most part, they have unostentatious good looks (though they are far less arresting than, say, Sarah Lawrence's frequently lush beauties).

The girls could have a carnival of dates, but the very availability of men, coupled with Harvard restraint, makes for an informal social pattern. Weekdays they get together in dorm parlors or talk over a cafeteria cup of coffee. Admittedly, Radcliffe girls are spoiled. Harvard freshmen are usually beneath notice for them; the lowliest Cliffie can command a senior, or even a graduate student.

Thirty-three of Radcliffe's 258 seniors last spring were married, which is a rather moderate figure. An unmarried senior described her graduate plans and added, "Subject to change, of course, if I become engaged."

There is still a vestige of the old blue-stocking spirit. While I was having lunch at Radcliffe, someone referred to a magazine story about a Harvard-Radcliffe romance. "Does it deal with a seduction?" I asked. "No," a girl snapped, "it deals with an *affair.*"

On a bright Sunday afternoon, I walked along the edge of the Charles River. The grassy slopes were speckled with blankets on which little knots of students reposed with their textbooks or copies of the *New York Times.* The students were largely segregated by sex. To my astonishment, the tableau froze. Very few Harvard boys left their small plot of real estate to sally forth into Radcliffe territory. In my mind's eye, I could see other campuses —Cornell, or Michigan, or Brooklyn College—where a similar challenge would evoke a far different response.

Harvard compensates for Radcliffe's numerical deficiencies by ransacking the resources of such local schools as Simmons, Wellesley, Emerson, and Boston University. But only the enterprising deserve the fair, and there are many Harvard boys for whom Saturday night is uncompanioned and joyless. Vivid in my mind are the two freshmen—at least they looked like freshmen—who lurched past me after what must have been a heroic consumption of beer. Arms around each other's shoulders, smiling, incoherently, they shambled into the night.

In counterpoint to Harvard's normal well-bred amiability, there is a thin line of outlaws and dissidents. One hears vaguely of Bohemian enclaves within the houses, but they never quite materialize. There is, however, a kind of genteel outpost of the Beat Generation in Cambridge. Espresso shops in the Greenwich Village pattern have begun to spring up, replete with candlelight, jazz trios, and bitter coffee.

For the most part, they are frequented by well-scrubbed couples out on a Friday night date. But they are also the spiritual haven for the Cambridge perennials, weary worldlings who have stayed in Cambridge after graduation. Vaguely writing a book, working part-time, or living off a trust fund, they float in some shadowy limbo between the B.A. and the wide, wide world.

According to one of the coffeehouse owners, a Brandeis alumna with a major in literature, the Clubbies react to Bohemianism with a jumpy truculence. The products of prep school and North Shore can evidently find black stockings and no lipstick un-

settling. There have been incidents. In one case, only the presence
of an ex-Clubbie, now disaffiliated and Beat, averted a nasty fight.
The ultimate in insouciance was reported by a coffeehouse which
had been broken into at four in the morning. The police found
a Clubbie, haughtily unmindful, having a leisurely cup of coffee
right in the middle of the shop.

Harvard has votaries aplenty. Van Wyck Brooks sees it as the
home of the inner-directed man, free from the "patent-leather
smiles" of his fraudulent contemporaries. A recent alumnus describes it as a place where "the Bronx High School of Science
finds itself flanked by Groton and St. Paul's." Its friends admire
its fostering of independence—Harvard indifference, they argue,
is a way of protecting independence—its unswerving pursuit of
excellence, its sustained defense of the "right to utter." (President
Pusey, of course, stood up to McCarthy with courage and dignity, which was no small feat at the time.)

Harvard asks not merely, "What are the facts?" but "What
do the facts mean?" Jonathan Kozol, a recent graduate, wrote:
"Whatever fine things may be said for the well-rounded, smoothly
adapted, broadly interested boy, something especially fine should
be said for the undistracted, wholly devoted, single-intentioned
student whose sole reason for being is to study long hours of
intent concentration."

To be sure, there is an antiphony of criticism. Harvard is
charged with being vast, impersonal, and amorphous ("many
spokes without a hub"). The faculty is Olympian and unap-
proachable. ("You don't feel they really want you to visit," a
student said.) The college's pride is overblown, some argue. "It's
like the Hegelian mystique of the state," a professor observed.
"People forget that there are values larger than the University."
Some ingrown types have even expressed resentment at the rise
to academic eminence of the University of California.

The most vigorous philippic against Harvard was provided by
a now defunct little magazine, the *Cambridge Review*. In a special
issue in 1956, it offered a sorehead view of Harvard and a garish
mix of ideas from Wilhelm Reich, Henry Miller, and John
Dewey. It assailed the "ritualistic inanities" of socal intercourse in
Cambridge, "the phony realism and fake maturity," and Harvard's

repression of the "lithe, natural movement of thought and feel-ing." It even committed the ineffable sin of admiring some features of Yale.

The editors sadly concluded: "The truth is we know so much we do not feel anything. . . . The University has forgotten that human beings help each other by interaction, by fighting and loving. Tutors and professors, if they are to live, must be involved with their students even in a latently sexual manner with the possibility of the sex becoming overt."

What distinguished this critique of Harvard, aside from its bizarre theory of togetherness-cum-sex, its occasional insights, and its barbarous misspellings, was its bland acceptance of Harvard's eminence. "Harvard's greatness as an educational insti-tution is being destroyed," it asserted. "This school cannot be called a school of *veritas*."

What does the future hold for Harvard? In 1958, the univer-sity was agitated by a bitterly waged fight over the refusal of George Buttrick, the University Preacher, to allow Memorial Church to be used for non-Christian ceremonies. Buttrick took the position that for a Christian church such a function was anomalous. President Pusey ultimately withdrew his support from this view, after a surge of disapproval from secularists, re-ligious indifferents, "village atheists," and some members of the Divinity School.

The controversy brought out some latent antagonisms to Pusey's emphasis on religion, but it was also suggested to me— not entirely facetiously—that in the eyes of some Harvard jingoes his real offense lay in *putting God above the college*. A campus wag rewrote the Ten Commandments with Harvard in the place of Jehovah.

The Harvard tradition is essentially Unitarian, but in recent years it has been dominated by scientism. Pusey in his assaults on secularism and in his espousal of the creative arts represents a countervailing tendency. (It has also been pointed out by some that his sacerdotal tone, in the early days at least, strengthened his hand against Senator McCarthy. In any case, the sequence of religiosity and anti-McCarthyism disconcerted his critics on both sides.)

Harvard is not displeased with its present way of life, but it is not settling into smug somnolence. At the moment there is ferment in the creative arts. A theater building was recently completed, and a center of design is contemplated for the future. The timing of Harvard's artistic renaissance is interesting. No weathervane to academic fashion, Harvard maintained its high intellectual standards while other colleges, under the rubric of self-expression and creativity, were watering theirs down. Having consolidated its intellectual gains, Harvard can now turn to the arts. Characteristically, its theater will remain extracurricular and will not be integrated with course work.

Rich but not *that* rich, Harvard recently beat the bushes for $82.5 million in order to expand its facilities, increase scholarships, and meet an anticipated boom in enrollment. Not too long ago, President Pusey announced that the fund-raising goal was exceeded with the help of alumni, including members of the exclusive "$100,000 Club."

Harvard Yard buffs will no doubt be distressed to learn that future architecture will be modern in design; there is no room to build except up.

Harvard contemplates its abundance with quiet pleasure. It has a right to. Imperial but modest, dignified but humorous, Harvard bestrides the American college scene—a well-mannered colossus.

ON WISCONSIN!

The casual visitor to Madison, Wisconsin, is often bemused by the sight of rival state capitols, a mile apart on the main thoroughfare. The loftier of these buildings bulks large behind a huge statue of Abe Lincoln, seated, brooding, and timeless. No state capitol, this is Bascom Hall, the antique nerve center of the University of Wisconsin, in many ways the prototype of the Big Ten and certainly one of the most vigorous examples of public higher education. The way the two capitols confront each other across a mile of department stores and dress shops is by no means fortuitous, for at Wisconsin the relationship between legislature and university is intimate, contentious, and fruitful. The university occupies the higher ground, and this, too, has symbolic overtones. "Madison is the only place where the academician looks down on the politician," an alumnus observed. And it is clear that no politician can propel his career by attacking the university. Even Senator McCarthy, at his snarling worst, refrained from taking on Bascom Hall, despite its history of liberalism at least equal to that of Harvard.

The University of Wisconsin, encompassing hill and wood and plain and fronting the waters of Lake Mendota, is a merging of dizzying polarities. It is a state institution with relaxed admission standards. ("Any high school graduate in the state who really wants to can shoulder his way in," an official admitted.) Nevertheless, it is one of America's great universities, with a Ph.D. production rate—the Dow-Jones average of the academic world—up among the leaders. Amiably schizophrenic, it is at once an intellectual center and a playground for adolescents with an indomitable appetite for fun. It is where rural Wisconsin meets urban sophistication. Beer cascades endlessly, as one might expect in Wisconsin. Yet at the Student Union, where 3.2 beer is dispensed, five times as much milk is consumed. At 10 A.M. huge farm boys sip containers of milk while waiting for their next class. UW is the seat of liberalism, and its academic freedom statement of 1894 still reverberates, but the supervision of student life is repressively mid-Victorian. (Here rural values triumph, and the gaunt presence of mythical Aunt Minnie of Kaukana is heeded.)

The collision of opposites engenders little comment. Last spring no one saw anything surprising in two adjacent art exhibitions at the Student Union. One was a cornball collection of Norman Rockwell's Americana; the other, a group of impenetrable and tortured canvases by German expressionists. At the Union, the Hoofers, stolid partisans of ski trail and mountain, are next door to as arty a theater crowd as can be found west of Chicago. The silos and pigpens of the School of Agriculture border the tennis courts alive with shapely girls in short-shorts. It is a school where fusty professors are football-happy, and the annual Military Ball must share the limelight with the annual *anti*-Military Ball. Its lake is legendary, but for much of the year it is locked in a Siberian winter. A final paradox: UW is in the heartland of America, but its personality is ineradicably European as well. The university has sturdy departments of Germanic and Scandinavian studies, and its new president, Conrad Elvehjem, is a proud member of the Ygdrasil Norwegian Literary Society.

In short, UW is an academic cosmos, where the enterprising student can find almost anything he wants. The statistics are awesome. To its 18,000 students on its Madison campus (13,000 undergraduates, 5,000 graduate students), UW offers a staggering 1,350 courses in 88 departments, ranging from the most crassly vocational (Office Procedures) to the most magnificently esoteric (Advanced Sanskrit). It has a physical plant worth more than $88 million, and its annual operating budget exceeds $62 million. One thousand scholars, out of a faculty of 3,000, hover over 1,500 research projects. Students from every state and 84 foreign countries jam its frat houses, dorms, and rooming homes. The main campus is so far-flung that there is a bus from the faculty parking lot to Bascom Hall. Its marching song, "On Wisconsin," is known to more millions than any other and has been endlessly pirated. Its Memorial Union has served as a model throughout the country. It used to have the best boxing team in the college world, although its male students are slow to anger.

The unique flavor of the school—the way citizen-student and administrator stand nose to nose—was reflected in a recent meeting of the Contemporary Trends class at which President Elvehjem was a speaker. A sport-shirted student got up and asked bluntly if friction between the president and Dr. Joshua Lederberg was responsible for the departure of the Nobel Prize winner to the promised land of Stanford University. This struck Dr. Elvehjem as an entirely reasonable question, and he explained Lederberg's departure in terms of shifting research interests.

The populist tradition at UW is strong. The chauffeur of former President Erwin Broun Fred used to work in the paintshop. When a call would come from the president, he would jump out of his overalls and into a business suit in order to drive the president to meet a sultan or another visiting dignitary. Nor is rank much heeded. Unlike many parvenu schools which are acutely rank-conscious, UW prefers the egalitarian "Mister."

Populism is also deeply imbedded in the "Wisconsin Idea," the conviction that the university belongs to the people and should render service to it—"a wedding of soil and seminar." This is expressed in extension centers (in places with vaudeville gag names like Sheboygan), in agricultural research stations, and in the university's resident artist, Aaron Bohrod, going on tours of the state talking art to farmers and their wives. As part of its extension service, the university will answer almost any question asked by a responsible citizen. The late Selig Perlman, professor of labor economics, said reverently, "Wisconsin civilized the United States." He meant such things as workmen's compensation and social security in which the state, under the leadership of university personnel, pioneered.

The Wisconsin Idea is housed institutionally in the Wisconsin Alumni Research Fund, a huge enterprise which subsidizes research in such disparate areas as antibiotics, mink reproduction, heart-valve repair, development of new cheeses, etc. Some revolutionary advances were achieved at UW—for example, dicumarol, an anticoagulant which allegedly saved former President Eisenhower's life. The Alumni Fund helps make Wisconsin one of the great research centers in the country.

The Wisconsin Idea is epitomized in Jim Wimmer, a twenty-four-year-old student who managed Gaylord Nelson's successful campaign for the governorship and was appointed the governor's executive secretary. A sociologist on campus was unable to see me because he was busy testifying at the state legislature in behalf of the Menominee Indians, who are in traumatic transition from federal to state control. The Wisconsin Idea is represented, too, by the history professor who does a radio broadcast throughout the state and on one occasion received a letter which stated succinctly: "Dear Professor . . . Please drop dead."

Wisconsin used to boast that it has more cows than people. UW, however, is no cow college. In fact, its "Ag" students are the new Organization Men of farming, headed for careers in food processing, farm machinery, or government service. Authentic bumpkins can be found among the short-course students in farming (noncredit), for whom only grade school education is required.

Social cartographers abound at UW, and some are quick to divide the students into Langdon Street (fraternity row), the dorm crowd, and the Independents. Langdon Street is identified with fun, anti-intellectual vigilantism, and a consumption of beer little less than heroic. The dorm students—most of them at the far end of the campus—are reputed to be small-town or rural, ingenuous, and intellectually unformed. Their typical majors are home economics, agriculture, and education. (Engineering students occupy an undefined limbo; it is not a chic major, but no one would suggest that it is easy.) The Independents (called GDI by Langdon Street—Goddamned Independents) spill out of rooming houses and apartments to oppose Langdon Street Philistia. They provide the soldiery of dissent on campus and man the few frail barricades of radical causes.

There is a sharp urban-rural dichotomy at UW. A sociologist summed up the rural ambiance: "The rural kids tend to be absolutist in matters of religion and family. They see divorce as an evil; they lean towards 'familism,' with relatives as part of the inner family. They are not really independent because of the extended family pattern. The university is expected to stand *in loco parentis*. We're really euchered into a semi-parent position."

Emeritus President Edwin B. Fred, who spent his boyhood on a Virginia farm and forty-seven years of his adult life as a member of the Wisconsin faculty, claims that after they have been on campus a year, it is impossible to tell a farm boy from a city sophisticate. But other observers demur.

A graduate assistant in English from New York City observed: "The urban students are more acute; they catch on faster. But they sometimes have a superficial brightness. Rural kids are ingenuous, friendly, and less artificial." They are also almost totally lacking in irony, and he described with amusement the Chicago girl who sits and smiles with an assured sense of superiority whenever he indulges in irony. Her smile says, "You and I get it, but the others surely don't."

Martha Peterson, the amiable and perceptive Dean of Women, observed that big-city girls with problems "have a big thing about going to the psychiatrist." On the other hand, to refer a small-town girl for therapy, "you have to sneak up on her."

The small-town girl sets modest goals. She is unlikely to think of a glamorous career in the State Department, and some with a four-point index (as close as you can get to scholastic charisma) are content to settle for elementary school teaching.

Miss Peterson tells of the occasion when she invited ten small-town dorm girls to a Sunday night supper at a friend's lake house. "We fed them well, and they ate beautifully," she recalled. "But we couldn't really get a conversation going except for some mild complaints about the food in the dorms. For the most part they sat around and read back copies of magazines." The next week Miss Peterson received ecstatic notes from the girls affirming what a marvelous time they had and telling how they had written home about the memorable evening.

There are striking differences in social life too. A rural boy came to a house-fellow and asked him for "some topics of conversation for a date." Another bucolic gallant is in the habit of carrying three-by-five cards with deft little conversational gambits neatly typed on them. Formals, in particular, scare them to death.

Sex morality has its rural and urban variations. Generally speaking, rural girls become involved in intimate relationships because of deep and solemn love. They are often appalled at the cavalier way some of the more sophisticated girls have affairs with only a mild affection or a hazily defined intellectual compatibility as sanction.

Carnal anarchy prevails no more at UW than at other universities. Certainly, the administration exercises a steely-eyed vigilance. (A recent satiric skit has the president saying: "I spend 90 per cent of my time regulating the sex life of students, football for the alumni, and parking for the faculty.") Nevertheless, in warm weather there are beaches and cars. In the winter, according to a dorm supervisor, "sex is more challenging." Satyrs don't gambol in Midwestern groves, but it would be naive to assume too much sexual quiescence. However, students feel little need to dramatize their sexual liberation. In fact, this generation of students is much given to trappings of virtue. A member of a big "social" frat said: "Oh, the boys talk about sexy girls. They like to take them out once or twice but don't want to go steady with them." And the women students, for the most part, are girdled in propriety. However, one girl, a free-wheeling Independent, observed tartly, "The vividness with which so many nice girls describe what happens to *other* girls would suggest that they're not as pure as they say."

Recently, a mass-circulation magazine featured a provocative article entitled "Are We Making a Playground Out of College?" In it, UW was severely castigated as a high capital of frivolity. *The Daily Cardinal*, UW's student newspaper, said ruefully: "We can see the looks on the faces of Grandma Jones and her neighbors in Superior, Sinsinawa, Silver Lake, and Spread Eagle when they read this week's *Post*." Then in a more vigorous spirit, the newspaper affirmed: "We've made Wisconsin a playground; it's up to us to reconvert it into an institution of higher learning." A student leader, however, declared: "I'm proud that we're a college playground. They refer to us as the dead generation, but the fact that we pull some of our humorous events is a distinguishing feature."

Other students, peering wistfully behind barricades of books, asked, "Boy, what have we been missing!" A young man in the student senate explained, "When visitors from Iowa come on a weekend, they tend to overdo things, because this is supposed to be a big play school. Students, however, don't go out on a nine-month bender." Then he pondered a moment and added judiciously, "Not unless they can adjust to it." "Adjust or drown," another boy said mirthfully as he hoisted his can of beer.

How much fun is enough? Has the university attained a balance between the life of ideas and extracurricular activity, or is the very notion of a great university sponsoring the elaborate apparatus of fun an absurdity? Some faculty members think so. "Our prestige goals are wrong; they're largely social," a professor said firmly. ("College professors everywhere think their students are stupid," an administrator countered.) This much is clear: the pursuit of fun is ubiquitous. There is little surcease from the relentless sequence of Homecoming (floats and parades), Humorology (skits), Campus Carnival, Haresfoot ("All our girls are men, and everyone's a lady"), weekends on lakes for which fraternities charter busses, dances, and parties, parties, parties. One of these was a "Pink and Blue Party" in which, in an unwitting parody of themselves, the boys came in blue, the girls in pink, "and they were all supposed to look like children."

There may be something amiss when only seven students turn up for academic freedom forum, while thousands mill around at Campus Carnival. (It is only fair to point out, however, that Dr. J. Robert Oppenheimer and Mrs. Eleanor Roosevelt drew capacity crowds when they gave talks.) Or it may simply be as one corn-fed girl remarked, "When we work, we work hard; when we play, we play hard."

This playfulness sometimes has an unexpected element of social criticism. The word "Mickey Mouse," UW argot for trivial, is constantly in use, as if the students are looking uneasily over their own shoulders. A few years ago, a naval ROTC unit was proudly doing close-order drill in a crowded stadium between halves of a big football game. Suddenly, out of Badger Block, the chauvinist cheering section, came a derisive song: "M-I-C-K-E-Y-M-O-U-S-E. That's the way you spell Mickey Mouse." Throughout the enormous stadium, students picked up the chant gleefully.

Fraternity and sorority row incurs a good deal of animus about UW's overdeveloped play habits, since the Greeks are the chief artisans of organized fun. And beer consumption is the hallmark of the fraternity man. (State Street leading away from Bascom Hall is lined with beer joints.) A girl from Sweden described beer parties as "just a huge noise." She explained, "You don't even get to know the boys because they're drunk before you even get settled." A sorority girl frowned at the mention of beer. "It gets to be an obsession with some boys," she said. "At a party I asked for a coke. My date was so embarrassed, he asked me to pour the coke into an empty beer can."

A frat boy, with a scrupulous sense of the fitness of things, said, "We wants lot of milk on the table during the week and lots of beer on Friday and Saturday nights."

I attended a fraternity party—liquid and raucous—in which the empty beer cans were placed neatly on top of one another in the shape of a pyramid. It mounted to the ceiling as the evening went on. Another party had a rock 'n' roll combo (Blackjack Corfines and his Hound-dogs), and couples twitched spasmodically to the music. At still another party, girls in drastically cut-down dungarees, and boys in overalls sang folk songs while the housemother sat in the next room reading a magazine.

UW students take a wry pride in having fathered the panty raid. There was also a small flurry of phone-booth jamming, some of it engineered by a local department store which offered prize money for a contest in front of the store. But UW's particular genius for horseplay expresses itself in the water fight. After Wisconsin comes the deluge. Students pelting each other with buckets of water may conceivably be some kind of Jungian fertility ceremony. It is certainly part of the rites of spring.

I arrived in Madison on a soft spring night, the first warm evening of the year. More than a thousand students milled around Langdon Street under the benevolent surveillance of the police. (In the old days they used to fire their pistols over the heads of the students.) Aside from some small skirmishes, a major dousing did not develop.

The students offered a persuasive rationale. They had endured a bitter winter. "You didn't know which was more confining," a student explained, "the four walls of your room or the snowbanks outside." Girls would get up in the morning, reach into their closets, and wear *everything*. (As a gesture of defiance at the weather, they continued to wear sneakers.) Springtime is the great liberation. People are friendlier; they can even say "Hello." (In the winter, their heads are bent against the wind.) Couples can hold hands without fear of frostbite. And the cracking of Lake Mendota, which had just taken place a few weeks before, was apparently sheer drama. There were hourly reports from ebullient students on the thunderous breaking of the ice. The water fights—"the annual virus" an official called it—are simply a response to the urge to do something that students feel on the first warm days.

To this the administration says a peremptory "No." And, curiously, in a school with a great libertarian tradition, the machinery of suppression is grim and ponderous. A few years ago, the fraternities "got the big knock" as a result of a riotous water fight, and were required to police themselves. On Langdon Street, during the abortive water fight, there were fraternity officers—a crew-cut Gestapo in Bermudas—taking names of frat men who were present.

Nevertheless, the drive against the aquatic Freedom Fighters is only partly successful. *Cardinal* gleefully reported that a dorm water fight in which wastebaskets, water cups, shoe boxes, and plastic bags were pressed into service, produced "the closest cooperation" attained by any function in that house. In a women's dorm—the girls are generally avid handmaidens in water warfare—trash cans were removed by the administration and holes punched in them to forestall their use as weapons. The hapless girls had to wait months for the trash cans to come back.

Water occasioned another controversy last spring. There was a furore last spring about the delay in setting up the piers along the shores of Lake Mendota. The administration wanted the fraternities to pledge that bodies wouldn't go hurtling into the deep.

"Residents do not realize the dangers inherent in mass dunking," an official stated primly. The students vociferously demanded their piers. When delay persisted, they prepared an effigy of one of the dorm supervisors with the legend, "Thanks for the piers." At the last minute, the effigy burning was averted. The pathos of the episode is that the object of their wrath was no martinet but one of the new breed of personnel technicians, desperately bent on "understanding" the students. The administration is now considering a kind of voluntary mass deportation. They hope to have old-fashioned launches carrying students on the lake at a nickel a ride from Langdon Street to the playing fields and Picnic Point. Their objective is to kill off Langdon Street's hegemony over organized horseplay.

There are some indications of a trend away from overblown fun. The Junior Prom, a venerable tradition at UW, was recently abolished. And an imposing symposium, organized around the theme "The Challenge of the Sixties," was a striking success and was well attended by students.

Social life at UW has characteristic *élan*. The girls, of course, are coolly marriage-conscious. The ratio of men to women—two to one—is helpful. ("I just wish they would admit it," a boy said testily.) The royal road to matrimony was outlined to me: lavaliered in the soph year; pinned in the junior year; engaged in the senior year. To be sure, there are anxieties. A sorority girl confessed that if she is dateless on Saturday night she hesitates to be seen on Langdon Street. A frat boy remarked that he is taunted by his brothers if he chooses to study on Friday evening. "I think it's a freshman's school," a sophomore girl said. "Freshman year is a big blast. You're a new face and it's all snow and beer and fraternities. Then when you're a sophomore you see the boys on the street, and it's just 'Hi.' In the meantime, they're looking over the new crop."

The Greeks and Independents glare at each other balefully. (The dorm crowd, though populous, is reputed to be out of things, insulated by a bucolic torpor.) The Independents watch the pageantry of play with awed disapproval. The fraternity houses strike them as indecently sybaritic—some are remarkably luxurious—or childish. (One frat house is ornamented with a toilet bowl and a Model T Ford at its entrance.) Sorority girls are stereotyped as trench-coated, short-haired, and rah-rah. "The sorority stuff," a Student Union activist observed, "is even more Mickey Mouse than the Union. Here are seventy-five girls who are automatically my friends because we all paid our dues." A literature student said dispassionately: "I see them all looking and talking alike. They're just interested in trivia. I suppose I am too, but their trivia are not mine." A graduate assistant in art made the telling point that the Langdon Street crowd are afraid to draw well in art class for fear of being outstanding. "It's the same in criticism," he added. "They hesitate to criticize each other."

The fraternity boys do their share of glowering. "The Independents are just people who don't fit into groups," one of them said. And an angry polemicist summed up the bohemian fringe: "They scorn conformity, yet they all look alike. Each gray face and each black-stockinged leg, and each uncombed head looks like every other. They scorn the tennis-shoed and beige trench-coated Bascom Hall cult without realizing that they are just as conformist."

The sexes occasionally snap at each other too. A girl wrote a letter to *Cardinal* lamenting the "lost, strayed, and/or probably extinct mature male." She appealed for someone "individual enough to wade barefoot in a puddle or walk down the street eating a double-dipped ice-cream cone . . . a conversationalist who doesn't have to rely on the latest adventures of *Maverick* or *Gunsmoke*."

A young man shrilled against the campus Messalinas who flaunt their charms in tight sweaters and skirts. "I'm in favor of clean, decent sex appeal," he expostulated, "but it's not one bit funny when a man can't even walk down a street without having his emotions unreasonably stimulated by females. Don't girls realize what their sexiness does to a man? Girls are not flowers which men merely desire to look at."

Sooner or later, everybody meets at the Memorial Union, the self-styled "living room" of UW. Occupied daily by about fourteen thousand people, it is at once cultural heart of the university, lounge, dining room, art gallery, workshop, forum, dance hall, meeting room, theater, and more. (It also has an ineffably

lovely lake-side dining terrace on the lake.) No student need stray
from campus, for the Union is both Parnassus and juke joint. On
a Saturday night last spring, the Dolphins (water ballet) were
splashing synchronously at one end of the campus; in the Union
actors were posturing elegantly in scenes from *The Importance
of Being Earnest;* and a costume dance was in progress in a ballroom, where a Burmese student did an interminable fire dance.
Meanwhile, the Rathskeller (invariably called "the Rat") churned
with talk, boy met girl in cavernous corners of the gloomy cellar,
the jukebox jumped, and all activity, solemn or gay, was well
lubricated by a steady flow of 3.2 beer—and milk.

The Rat is the hangout for bearded rebels, sandaled folk singers,
and foreign students, as well as for small-town types enthralled by
the colorful outlanders. But despite a lot of official rhetoric about
the more than nine hundred foreign students, all is not well. A
campus survey revealed that though students are willing to live
in the same house with members of minority groups, they are
reluctant to date them. Over half would not date a Negro or
Oriental; a third side-steps social contact with Latin-Americans.
Not unexpectedly, fraternity and sorority people are less tolerant
than others.

"If that boy from India calls, I'm not in," a girl left word with
her roommate. Others date foreign students as an adventure in
exoticism. "Did you see who I was with last night?" they then
ask their friends.

The bulletin boards proclaim the teeming diversity of campus
life. Under the sign for the Annual Military Ball (ROTC formal)
is the announcement of the third annual anti-Military Ball (informal with recorded music) whose theme is "The Street Where
You Lived, or Dig You Later, Atom Crater." The anti-Military
Ball's attendance doubled not long ago (from 200 to 400) and was
enlivened by an attempted kidnapping of their leaders as a re-
prisal for the kidnapping, by parties unknown, of a guard at the
Military Ball. Even grave political issues begin to sound like something out of an old-fashioned college musical at UW.

A friend of mine who leafed through *The Badger,* UW's yearbook, gasped incredulously, "My God, it's a Sears, Roebuck catalogue!" Indeed, students respond in much the same way to the

profusion of activity. One said, "The nice thing is that you can walk out on a group, and it will still be there when you want it." Another observed, "Wisconsin offers a real-life situation. It has everything—even an Oberlin if you want it." (In the Midwest, Oberlin is considered a prairie Harvard.) The *everything* includes a quaint UW game or dance called "limbo," in which a boy or girl, by bending his knees and arching his back, inches under a rope while everyone chants, "Limbo, limbo, limbo." A shapely girl remarked matter-of-factly, "A more seductive routine for a girl has yet to be choreographed."

UW, of course, is the home of Big Football. Even serious students respond to the zip and sparkle of a football weekend. One professor described football as the only real communal activity at the university, and he spoke with genuine affection of the march to the stadium ("Nobody would think of driving.") To the highly sophisticated, football is a kind of secret vice publicly enjoyed. No intellectual will openly espouse it though he may attend all the games.

A professor who grew up in the Midwest defined his attitude: "I like football. I like the pageantry. But colleges ought to hire good football teams and stop pretending the game has anything to do with education." One faculty member suggested that the Chicago Bears be hired as artists-in-residence.

President Elvehjem pointed out that the athletic budget is a modest million dollars against $15 million for research. "When you have 18,000 students on campus and no football to let off steam, you'll have more panty raids." As for the drive to win (1960 record: 4–5), the football coach wants the team in the top ten to keep it even with the university's academic standing.

The coaching staff, by the way, shrewdly resists the impulse towards punditry so characteristic of coaches at other schools. (The attraction of the life of the mind for muscle-merchants has long been underestimated.)

Football players have become seriously devalued in recent years. They are Saturday's children, neglected the rest of the week. No longer heroes, they are just hulking mercenaries to many students. "Animal farm" was the scornful epithet of one student. A huge 6'5" linesman ("They're not all as big as me") studied his bruised hands and spoke of the plight of the gladiators: "I think students look down on football players as animalistic. And maybe we are. Other people can sit at their desks, but we have to keep moving. You know, we'll be walking up the hill, and suddenly we'll start shoving each other."

Some years ago, before the wider world beckoned, it was a ritual for many Brooklyn College students to attend UW's summer session to savor the delights of an out-of-town school. The idea of a lake on campus—swimming between classes—seemed deliciously frivolous after the gray austerities of a subway school.

A Brooklyn College girl, darkly pretty and intense, wrote of her experience last summer: "Such things are not for you, I said to myself. You'll prance off to Brooklyn College (with its fine faculty), major in education, marry, have a boy and a girl, and become President of Hadassah. You'll never room with a girl from Kalamazoo and fight off a Lutheran from Texas. You'll never have coffee with an Ethiopian whose father is in the UN, discuss Israel with an Arab, and segregation with a Negro from the South." Her own impact on UW was almost as dramatic as its own on her. She described a moment of sheer Gauguinesque splendor when, after a swim, she shook out her lustrous black hair. "The boys just went wild," she wrote. "They looked at me as if an electric shock passed through their bodies."

What about the intellectual life at UW? Estimates vary. A recent study reveals that the university, despite its open-house philosophy, is getting higher-ranking students from high schools than do the country's colleges as a whole. (In 1959, 60.7 per cent of the freshmen were from the top quarter of their class, while only 2.7 per cent were from the bottom quarter.) Fred Harvey Harrington, the able vice-president in charge of academic affairs, said flatly, "Students are better academically than they were."

The range of ability is wide. According to an informal estimate by an English professor, one-third of the students have difficulties in expressing themselves. The faculty chants dolorously about the intellectual insufficiencies of their students. "I gave an exam and used the word 'expendable,' " one man reported. "A number of students asked what it meant."

But it is the flaccidity of intellectual life that grieves the faculty.

"It's difficult to get them to talk," a distinguished teacher of literature observed. "They're so accustomed to a passive role. You have to pull it out of them. They submit to authority; they hesitate to risk their intelligence. It's almost as if they were painted on the wall." Then he added compassionately: "I often think there are too many of them and too few of us."

A girl made a bold assertion about mass education in one of her courses. Her instructor challenged her thesis. "I take it back," she said meekly.

A social scientist complained about intellectual quietism on campus: "They don't inquire about religion. There is an organized religious structure, and they accommodate themselves to it. They take for granted that they're going to be married—and married soon. This represents a decline in individuality, for when you marry you limit your individuality. You take on a conservative component.

"They simply don't feel enough. The job of the social scientist is to get people to think objectively about subjects for which they feel some passion. But these kids are not impassioned about anything."

There is, to be sure, a free commerce of ideas on campus. Recently a Marxist ideologist spoke to students about racial segregation, and shortly thereafter a priest advanced "Christian arguments for capitalism" to the members of the Conservative Club. It is UW's proud boast that it was the last college campus to maintain a chapter of the Labor Youth League, an allegedly Communist-front group. (Former President Fred fought the American Legion on this issue.) The small group finally died of inanition, and the shriveling-up process was no doubt accelerated by the student handbook which let students know that LYL was on the Attorney-General's list. Both the students and the administration opposed loyalty oaths in connection with the National Defense Education Act.

Student intellectuals fall into at least four elites: the New Idea group (editors of the literary magazine, who, according to one critic, "have not budged an inch from the avant-garde"); foreign intellectuals; scientists; and fraternity boys with a taste for ideas, who have tired of frat-house fatuities. (One professor asserts that there are many intellectuals immured in a kind of cozy concentration camp on Langdon Street. "Our job should be to help them break out," he said.)

The Green Lantern, an eating co-op, is one of the more spirited intellectual enclaves. Reputed to be vaguely leftist and aggressively bohemian, its members are full of a strident but cheerful insurgency—not without a sly consciousness of the absurdity of some of their postures. Raffish, Saroyanesque, they hunch over cigarette-scarred tables in their cooperative cave (the co-op is in a cellar) and intone slogans for new crises. The hard core is from New York, shaggy-headed and fiercely intellectual, wise-guy heirs of the dead wars of the thirties. Around them are a few pretty girls, surfeited with the inanities of Langdon Street, and some small-town boys awed by the sheer articulateness of these avatars of protest. ("They come as Taft conservatives and leave as socialists," one of the ideologists said.) Nevertheless, one boy called me stealthily by phone to protest his innocence of the heresies I heard expressed. He was opposed, he said, to creeping socialism, which would suggest that the contagion of ideas has limits. " I go there only because the food is cheap," he explained.

The Green Lantern denizens express themselves with aphoristic pungency. Football: "We sit on the steps and watch the parade of citizens go by. Then we listen to the roar." ROTC: "You march up and down in the Quonset Hut, and guys with little stripes yell at you." Fraternities: "They metabolize a lot, but their ends are trivial." Wisconsin boys: "Naive but very decent; free from the oppressive neurosis of New Yorkers." Themselves: "We're not rebels; we all had happy childhoods." They even have a social chairman to betoken their normalcy.

Particularly exhilarating are visits by candidates for office in student government. These poor innocents are badly roughed-up by the cerebral hoods of the Green Lantern.

The final word, however, belongs to a Wisconsin girl who fled the joys and terrors of the co-op. "I could stand the talk," she explained, "but I couldn't endure the dirt."

No doubt, the most talked-about student at UW was Richard S. Wheeler, *The Cardinal's* acidulous commentator on manners and morals. An unabashed student of Mencken, Wheeler assailed the liberal pieties in a prose of unusual trenchancy. The students seemed to take a curious pleasure in the pummeling they receive. "The notorious Wheeler," a student called him, and another gravely explained that Wheeler is bitter "because the Midwest isn't like the East where he once lived."

"The trouble with fraternities," Wheeler wrote at a time when the university passed the 1960 clause outlawing discrimination, "is not that they are undemocratic but rather not aristocratic enough." He dismissed idealism as "a malignant tumor of adolescence . . . a kissing cousin of superstition and fantasy." He raised hackles with a column on necking: "Every time a young lady necks, she's taking a lesson in frigidity. . . . A half-hour's sabbatical in the bathroom with a good book is infinitely more pleasurable." After the piece appeared, he received calls from irate young men whose erotic maneuvers had been repulsed by young ladies brandishing Wheeler's column.

Wheeler also did deadpan interviews with Badger beauties to "make them look like the dumb blondes they usually are." One guileless doll prattled on in this fashion: "I think psychology is so interesting. One professor has a wonderful theory, and at the end of the semester you really believe him, and then next semester another professor refutes everything. I would say that psychology is a science . . . it's good, but it has its bad aspects too." Another beauty confessed: "I was thinking of attending Radcliffe, but it's unnatural. All those girls living just for their weekends. That's not moral."

The faculty at UW is considered strong and no more factious than most. Salaries are good but not good enough. The average for a full professor is $11,069; associate professor, $8,288; assistant professor, $6,827; instructor, $5,614. The campus, described as "sublime" by a visiting Englishman, is supposed to be worth easily $1,000 a year, but assent to this quaint notion by faculty is not easily obtained. Nevertheless, many faculty people, modest salaries notwithstanding, live in handsome suburban developments. There are even some futuristic homes which make East Coast suburbia look timid and unadventurous.

The strongest departments are biochemistry and history. There is some uneasiness among the arts people about the research boons that scientists have for the asking. There was the hope that after President Fred, a man in the humanities or social sciences would be elevated to the presidency in a kind of rotation. (Elvehjem is a biochemist who has done distinguished work in vitamin B-1 complex.) Nevertheless, there has not been too much grumbling about research money. A normal teaching load is three courses a week (nine teaching hours), and the university expects scholarly output from its faculty.

"Formally, we are slaves; factually, we are free men," the late Selig Perlman explained. The price of freedom in a university is the evermultiplying body of faculty committees. "Spending all your time milling around is a consequence of faculty democracy," Vice-President Harrington explained. (Psychologist Carl Rogers, father of nondirective counseling, had to be approved by ten committees when he was appointed recently.) A solution to all this backing and filling is to cut down on the size of committees and their functions. This is currently being considered.

Faculty members range from strenuously informal types in sport shirts and tennis shoes to a Harvard Ph.D. in pencil-thin tie, scrupulously narrow suit, and a faintly supercilious manner, who seems determined to maintain an outpost of gentility among the corn cribs. Careerism rockets along at UW, and relief is in sight only when one is a full professor with tenure. There is also fierce intercollegiate rivalry for academic talent, and former President Fred used to keep a scoreboard of faculty people who went to the University of Michigan—the big rival—and vice versa.

UW has a Midwestern bonhomie. A man who taught at the University of Chicago asserts that there is far more communication among departments at UW. Nor is there any of the usual churlishness directed against the School of Education, since letters and science faculty members vote on all matters pertaining to that school, and there are joint appointments to both schools; for instance, a history professor will also teach the history of education. There is even a measure of good will towards deans. "At least they're scholars and researchers," a faculty member said grudgingly.

I talked with a sociologist, full of that ponderous jargon without which the social scientist feels undressed. After discussing "well-structured family interactional patterns," he turned to life in Madison and plunged into a racy and uncluttered idiom. "Boy, this town's a drag," he said. "Occasionally, my wife and I want to get something to eat late at night, but Madison folds up at 1 A.M. On New Year's Eve there are the same people counting noses to see who is at whose party."

There are hundreds of graduate assistants at UW who lead a strangely amphibian existence. They often teach sections for professors with whom they, in turn, take courses. Moreover, though they have faculty status, they take upper-division courses with undergraduates.

Being a graduate student means the big change from directed to autonomous study. ("You grow up overnight.") It also involves a search for an academic father—a professor in the student's area of scholarship. Relationships are close, and there are very few students languishing for years while sweating out their Ph.D.

Teaching can be vexatious for graduate assistants. Some status-minded undergraduates test them arduously before final acceptance. Then there is often a lack of coordination between quiz sections and the big lecture section. "But Mr. Whitley said at the lecture . . ." Often, Mr. Whitley said nothing of the kind.

It is characteristic of UW as an open society that the phone numbers of faculty members, and their addresses, are published in a directory available to all students. Students phone at all hours of the day and night—sometimes for the flimsiest of reasons.

How effective are graduate assistants? An argument in their behalf is that they make small classes possible. Nor are they all neophytes. Many have taught elsewhere, and the great concentration is between the ages of twenty-six and twenty-eight. President Elvehjem asserted baldly: "Some are very good. I think I did some of my best teaching when I was a graduate assistant."

It was former President Fred who observed that it is UW's unique habit "to haul all our dirty linen in front of Abe Lincoln's statue and wash it in public." In recent years, the proposal to erect a new building in Bascom Woods, near the famed carillon tower, provoked a spirited controversy. Everyone had his say—the woods are sacred—and the building plan finally squeaked through by a narrow margin. The university's grandiose building program has generated some student resentment. The new Chadbourne Dormitory, eleven stories of Miami Beach décor with a huge "W" on top, was quickly tagged the Chadbourne-Hilton. "How much is the university going to waste?" a sullen student asked.

A long-term student campaign to end compulsory ROTC was successful in 1960, and with voluntary military training came a new curriculum that became a pattern for ROTC throughout the country. Under it a good share of the instruction is in academic subjects, such as geography, military history, and speech, given by the university's own faculty, not by armed forces officers.

But the most acrimonious dialogue had to do with apartment regulations and the supervision of student life. "Apartment living is new and will increase," an official pointed out, "but the rules are old and outmoded." In truth, they smacked unpleasantly of a police state. A student living in a building into which an unmarried woman moved was required to move out. A forty-five-year-old New Zealander lived in the same building as a seventy-one-year-old woman. Hailed before the Student Conduct Committee, he protested, "Really, I had no designs on her." A student living in an apartment was required to report a roommate who entertained a female. ("But I was asleep," a boy protested.) This rule, to be sure, was contemptuously ignored.

After considerable debate, the faculty finally relaxed its vigilance and allowed entertaining in apartments without chaperones. But with its decision, it issued a warning that students must accept full responsibility for apartment life.

There was a fuss a few years ago over whether or not the university has the right to discipline a student for misbehavior in his home town during the summer vacation. A faculty member suggested the commonsense policy of "When they're off the hill, the hell with them." He added: "We're not in the business of building character. I doubt if some of us are qualified. Instead we should be concerned with building minds." Perhaps the ultimate in official doubletalk was attained by an administrator who declared piously: "I believe that when the average student comes to the University of Wisconsin, he is old enough to accept responsibility but young enough to need guidance."

The university views itself—its progress and grandeur—with

uneasy pride. UW is so ambitiously extended that the new shibboleth on campus is balance: between teaching and research, between undergraduate work and graduate study, between the liberal arts and professional education, between service to the state and service to the nation. How to establish a sound alignment of parts is an administrator's nightmare.

Maintaining quality in a school determined to give everyone a chance is also a headache. The fact that eight state schools have changed over from normal schools to four-year colleges may, in the future, drain off weaker students who would otherwise come to UW. The university now gives advanced standing to particularly able high school graduates, and it is instituting an honors program—but with a peculiarly egalitarian twist. "Our hope is to help gifted students without tagging them," the president stated. "Our bright people will learn by rubbing shoulders with average ones."

A great tradition is a burden as well as a joy. Has Wisconsin already had its great day? "There is little doubt that it lost some of its fire between the wars," Vice-President Harrington said. "There was a deflation of idealism, and other states began to originate things." At present there is a resurgence, but to attain distinction in a highly competitive period is another matter. UW people cast a troubled look at the West where the University of California—the General Motors of higher education—has been raiding faculty remorselessly. "Our problem," Harrington said, "is to see if we can keep the two dozen or so innovators on campus."

The University of Wisconsin grew out of a noble vision. "There is something extraordinary about Wisconsin," an administrator said. "After all, it's just an ordinary little state, its population no larger than that of Brooklyn. Yet this small state has created a great university."

At the conclusion of his inaugural address, President Elvehjem declared, "Give us, then, the hills to climb and the strength to climb them." Students wheezing up Bascom Hill would no doubt find this funny, but they too have been touched by the vision.

CLAREMONT: California's
Multicollege Campus

To some people Southern California is a neon world of hamburger stands, screwball religious sects, used-car lots, and starlets. But tucked away amid the strident tastelessness are tidy little communities more reminiscent of New England than of Southern California. Claremont, thirty-five miles east of Los Angeles, is such a town. Snuggled against the magnificent San Gabriel Mountains, it used to be all sagebrush and rattlesnakes and orange groves. The only concession it makes to the region is the restrained Spanish architecture of its pastel-tinted houses sparkling in the sunlight.

California—dizzy with growth and the home of the fresh start—has begotten in Claremont a plan to meet the burgeoning needs of higher education. Its answer is the Associated Colleges at Claremont, a federation of independent colleges grouping together for common advantages. Typically Californian in its confident facing-up to future growth, Claremont is far from worshiping size for its own sake. It is wedded to a New England ideal of quality—to be attained through small schools and its work ethos is as unsparing as that of Amherst or Harvard.

The Associated Colleges now number five, and acreage has been earmarked for additional schools. Dr. Robert J. Bernard, who told me the story of the founding of these colleges, a rugged man in his sixties, was named president of Claremont College in 1959 after serving the colleges in various roles since 1925. With a visionary gleam in his eyes and the indomitable energy of a wagon-train leader, Dr. Bernard talks with a robust optimism refreshing in a time of almost universal whimpering in education circles.

"No period in American history has a monopoly on founding," he said vigorously as he pointed out to me acres of sagebrush where new schools will rise. "It's been the thrill of my life to see the birth of new colleges. There is nothing to be undone here; we start from scratch." He recalled that President Lowell of Harvard had said to Dr. James A. Blaisdell, the founder of the Associated Colleges idea, "We can't do it, but you can in California." And in Claremont, with its lush gardens, its broad, calm streets, and the benign sunshine washing over everything, the Earthly Paradise shimmers around the next turn of Highway 66, where only twenty years ago Okies, sullen with want, went silently past in battered cars.

The Group Plan at Claremont is an arrangement in which a number of colleges share a common campus and certain common facilities—auditorium, library, and health center—and yet maintain their own autonomy. The rationale is that the colleges can remain small and preserve their own peculiar genius. At the same time, the advantages of a university are there at least in germ: the faculties and students can stimulate each other if they like, students can take courses at other schools, and the colleges can do things together they could not do alone—graduate courses, concert series, etc. (In effect, through their house plans, Harvard and Yale follow this pattern.)

The complex administrative structure has attracted wide interest among professionals; a local joke has it that any student who can explain the modus operandi of the Associated Colleges automatically gets a degree. The federation idea smacks of that hopeful American tendency to make the best of two worlds. But it was the example of Oxford University that inspired the experiment. Claremont is sometimes called the Oxford of the Orange Belt, and appropriately, Honnold Library has the largest collection of Oxfordiana this side of the Atlantic. Pomona's president, a former Rhodes Scholar, is editor of the *American Oxonian*.

The first college of the Claremont group was coeducational Pomona, founded in 1887. By 1925 population pressures forced it to decide whether to limit its enrollment or take in a horde of students clamoring at its gates. The answer was the Group Plan. Claremont College and then Scripps College for women were organized first. A men's school was projected, but the depression and World War II intervened. Expansion began in earnest in 1947 with Claremont Men's College; and Harvey Mudd College opened its doors for science and engineering in 1957. The capital in this academic federalism is Claremont College, the graduate and coordinating school headed by Dr. Bernard. Faculty from all the schools teach its courses; it administers the common facilities, and is charged with bulldozing new colleges into existence.

The casual onlooker sees a vast barony of academia at Claremont—500 acres, a mile and a half of academic workshop and bedroom and lounge. This astonishing profusion of building and campus caters to the needs of only 2,000 students in all. Someone from the East can contemplate its sheer spaciousness only with envy. (Brooklyn College, for example, ministers to the needs of 20,000 students on a paltry 42 acres.) The colleges have total resources, private in origin, of over $60 million.

The apologetics for the Group Plan is cheerfully contradictory. Each college has its own board of trustees for its special interests, but a central board of trustee presidents assures central control. Deans become as common as gardeners—and no more awesome. "You see, it's the law of diminishing utilities," a political scientist explained. "When there are so many administrators, no single one can be terribly important. It means that all these wretched deans are put in their place."

It may be that only in the euphoric logic of California can numbers mean, at once, enhanced strength and reduced strength.

Under the Group Plan students in any one college may take some courses offered in the others, and those available are listed in each catalogue. Pomona, the Big Daddy of the group, sometimes shies away from equality with its offspring. It has its own newspaper and news service and used to dominate in athletics. Since the fall of 1958, there have been two organized athletic programs, with the intention of giving more students a chance to play. The first football game between Pomona and the Claremont Men's and Harvey Mudd joint team was a rousing success this fall.

Claremont effectively refutes the glib idea that college students are the same from coast to coast. Each college has its own personality, and students learn early in the game about the prevailing stereotypes from their upper-class sponsors. Even the presidents—all Ph.D.'s with a background of college teaching—show these differences too. Pomona has perhaps the most formal head in Dr. E. Wilson Lyon; while at Scripps, Frederick Hard, gracious and courtly in manner, represents the Southern scholarly tradition. The heads of Claremont Men's College and Harvey Mudd are the new breed of college president—determinedly informal, youthful in manner if not in years. Jo Platt of Harvey Mudd—no one over the age of twenty-one calls him anything else—plays the guitar and sings academic ballads for his students. George Benson at CMC has the engaging air of a branch manager of an insurance company, and issues epistles to the unconverted full of brisk common sense. ("Does your talk at the family dinner table turn as often to literature as it does to snow in the mountains, Volkswagens, and the price of beef?")

California youth was recently described as "big, bronzed, and beautiful." To this observer they seemed indistinguishable from college students everywhere, who tend to be well nourished, cheerful, and only passing fair. Despite high academic standards, life is agreeable for Claremont students. The Pacific Ocean is only an hour away, and so is Palm Springs. Male students out on a tear will push on to Las Vegas, where one proud covey of CMC men was photographed with strip-tease artist Tempest Storm. But the gaudy glories of Hollywood are remote from the even tenor of life at Claremont. Some years ago when Clark Gable, hurtling by on Route 66, stopped at a student eating place to buy cigarettes, the Scripps girls poured out of their dorms.

Informality is an article of faith with California students, strenuously inculcated in high school. "I'm from California, and we're informal," a young man said to me with what amounted to truculence. Students are prone to drop in casually on their professors and perch on their desks. With a few regional variations dress at Claremont is that of the collegiate mass man—the boys in crew-cuts and Ivy League clothes, the girls short-haired and trim, in sensible college garb or Bermudas. At present, they said, there is a big thing with "go-aheads," Japanese sandals which fall off if one walks backwards.

A kind of domesticated beatness prevails. Jazz has many devotees, and *The Associated,* one of the local newspapers, goes in for a curious argot made up of hipster chatter, local idiom, and adolescent bravado. The report of a recent escapade began: "Herf, the steel baron, and Sheets made it up to watch the sweaty sweethearts of Grace Scripps take off a few tons tumbling. Since it was past pad-time, the portals were padlocked. . . ."

But beatness does not connote any flagging of vital energies. I watched an interfraternity track meet. The same boys I had seen sitting in class, loutishly uneasy, displayed a heroic energy on the track field. In a bicycle relay one husky kid took a spill that would have hospitalized a fullback. He rose out of a cloud of dust and blood and tried to mount the bicycle. It was twisted hopelessly out of shape by the violence of the fall. Little daunted, he picked the bicycle up, tucked it under his arm, and took off in pursuit of the pack on foot.

Slang is Claremont's lingua franca. "Jazzed" means feeling good, while "unjazzed" means depressed. "To mouse" is to neck. The Religious Center is "God's Office," and the area in front of the library is the "park of rest and culture." A "wimp" is a grind, dismally unathletic. Perhaps the raciest bit of patois is the oft-heard line, "Let's go check the bods in the fishbowl." Translated into more sedate prose it means, "Let's go to the glass-enclosed reference room in Honnold Library and look over the girls." Scripps girls complain that local boys, linguistically stunted, respond to almost anything with "Were you?" or "Don't you?" or "All the time."

The closest thing to a common campus for all the schools is The Wash, forty acres of sagebrush and serpentine dirt road—and, at night, parked cars. It is the unofficial "mousing" and drinking area. "On a busy Saturday night," a wise-guy student remarked, "you need a traffic cop."

Pomona College started in 1887 in the small town of Pomona, then faltered. When a real-estate boom in neighboring Claremont ("the leading town-site on the great Santa Fe route") fell apart, the Claremont Hotel, small and unfinished, was offered to the struggling school. It is now Sumner Hall.

Pomona was organized as a "Christian college of the New England type" by Congregationalists—the denomination which founded Harvard and worked on west, pulling out when a college was well launched. It has been described as the Swarthmore of the West—or as the best college south of Reed and west of Oberlin. It has a fistful of distinctions; the third Phi Beta Kappa chapter in the state; the highest percentage of graduates in *Who's Who in America* in California; fifth place among colleges in 1945–1955 in the winning of Woodrow Wilson Fellowships.

These attainments are likely to be announced in a slightly Southern accent, for the president and most of the deans are Southern. A sociologist at Pomona suggested that Southerners make skillful deans because they have a strong sense of community, and a college *is* an academic community. The handling of the liquor problem is distinctly Southern, according to this observer. Drinking is officially outlawed, but the deans expect students to drink—discreetly. Southerners are accustomed to walk a tightrope between conviction and expediency (thus, their pre-eminence in politics). Students, however, want none of this and dig in for a last-ditch fight for principle.

Pomona, is a traditional liberal-arts college with one thousand students and is regarded as the most grimly intellectual of all Claremont's schools. Status, in some measure, is determined by graduate plans (more than 60 per cent do graduate work), and even girls feel pressure to continue. "The real heroes among the students," President Lyon stated, "are those who get the big awards—the National Science, Danforth, and Woodrow Wilson Fellowships." This academic status-seeking has its critics. "You study for grades, not ideas," an articulate girl observed. "Grad schools aren't interested in ideas but in your grades."

Pomona's staff is a good one—so good, in fact, that President Lyon observed, "Between the research grants and the Fulbright Fellowships it's hard to keep our faculty on campus." One industrious statistician came up with the fact that the faculty had studied in, or visited, eighty foreign countries.

Among Pomona's recent innovations are two science buildings that rival any in the nation's liberal-arts colleges, and the student-operated radio station, KSPC, which broadcasts good programs to the whole Los Angeles area.

Pomona is coed; its neighbor to the north, Scripps College, is for girls. Pomona boys watch the nervous competition between the two groups of girls with smug pleasure. Folklore has it that Pomona boys date Scrippsies but marry Pomona girls. The standard gag, before students became motorized, was that you dated a Scripps girl because in the tired, stale hours of Sunday morning, all you had to do was roll downhill to get home. The stereotype is that the Scrippsy has a dainty, ladylike quality, while the Pomona girl is ferociously intellectual, barefoot, even disheveled. A Pomona girl said, "We feel like bulls in a china shop at Scripps. We're large and gross. We knock over vases." But I noticed that the Pomona and Scripps girls have one thing in common: the California girl's firm handshake and the tendency to talk first in social contact.

These stereotypes have even been built into regulations. Bermudas may be worn in Honnold (the central library), but sartorial propriety is required in the Scripps Library. Honnold is a teeming pick-up center, while the Scripps Library is an austere workshop with stained-glass windows and a dim, religious light.

The encircling intellectualism at Pomona means no enfeeblement of play. The student-guitar ratio is said to be as high as the student-faculty one. One whimsical boy leaves his classes through the windows. A professor found his office furniture ingeniously tied to the ceiling. Three fraternities have mountain cabins for high altitude carousing (forbidden by regulations but circumvented by nominal alumni ownership). The junior class had an outing on Mt. Baldy and went drinking its merry way up and down the ski lift. "It was," a boy recalled, "very warm on the inside and cold on the outside."

Local nursery games include "mudholing" (freshmen and sophs pelt each other with mud); Women's Play Day (hula hoops and tricycles); and "Measuring In" (an anatomic Saturnalia with a sociological twist—the girls are measured to prove that "the Pomona girl is not a stereotype").

I attended a reception for graduating seniors. It was all conscientious smiles and talk about future plans. Suddenly, a young man revealed a trustee's boast about having finally hired a political science professor who was a Republican. (They are evidently pretty scarce.) There was a nervous titter, and then President Lyon said somewhat magisterially, "The faculty and administration select the faculty—not the trustees."

Later, I attended an interfraternity beer party in one of the canyons. We got into a car and snaked up a mountain road. There were hundreds of students in shaggy outdoor garb, many of them kneeling before beer kegs like supplicants before druidic gods. Great heaps of food were being dispensed. Here and there a couple had climbed up a ridge and sat quietly in the waning sun, the girl with inclined head as she listened to a boy expostulate bitterly about a classroom injustice, a balky term paper, trouble in the fraternity.

There was one scar in this gentle landscape. A few boys from one fraternity were drunk. Two were rolling on the ground near the rim of the cliff, pummeling each other. A third was grandiloquently intoning, "Drunkenness and violence . . . that's our fraternity . . . drunkenness and violence." The girl friend of one of these boys turned to me. They were, she explained, really good, warm-hearted boys, with a great joy of life. It was the others—the dour scholars, the grinds—who were destroying them. There was no place at Pomona for them, and this was the only way they could protest. Near us, on the edge of the cliff, the sensitive thugs continued to roll in the dust.

Scripps College (two hundred and fifty students, faculty of forty-three) is a kind of cloistered Sarah Lawrence, without the social reformism and the commitment to experience that sends Sarah Lawrence girls pell-mell to field work in Puerto Rico and Canada. (Local students call Scripps "The Monastery" or "The Great White Wall.") What it has in common with its suburban New York counterpart is a girlish reverence for great works and a serious involvement in the creative arts. "This is not a Saks-Fifth-Avenue kind of school," an administrator remarked. But, in truth, the perfume-laden air of a finishing school does hover faintly over the Scripps campus. This is not to suggest that the girls are empty dolls or vague dilettantes. There are thousands of strenuous hours in the humanities program, and there can be genuine aesthetic fulfillment in a well-wrought urn.

The physical setting is a fantasy of patrician ease: grassy lawns, rows of lemon and orange trees, and even a "cutting garden," brilliantly abloom, so that the girls can snip fresh flowers for their rooms. There are numerous cool, tree-shaded courts with fountains and statuary. A high school senior, out to case the place, was startled to see a bevy of girls, their feet dangling in a fountain, taking an exam under the auspices of the honor code.

The atmosphere is compounded of quiet decorum (the girls dress for dinner) and academic earnestness. It is a gentle place, so gentle that there are two grades of F—a soft F, which can be redeemed into a D after appropriate academic penance, and a despairing FF, which can only be made up by repeating the course.

The heart of Scripps is the humanities program—three years of double courses for all, comprising two-fifths of the student's work during those years. The first year deals with the ancient world, the second with the Middle Ages and the Renaissance, and the third with the modern era. At the very least, the Scripps girl is likely to know a little about a lot. There is even a fighting chance that she will know a lot about a little. During her second year, the student takes an intensive seminar in a limited area. She also does a research paper, which gives her a chance, a Scripps brochure states, "to know this abbot or that artist . . . to put on the bones of any one of a thousand general statements about the past the flesh of the particular."

In her senior year each student does a senior thesis or project. An art major did a study of "Ceramics in Medieval England," which itself looked like a medieval manuscript. She used parchment and India ink and wrote in pseudo-medieval calligraphy. (She was aided by a remarkable collection of medieval manuscripts to which students have easy access.) Some girls go in for a relentless integration of fields. A student interested in French and drama chose a one-act play by Anouilh, translated and adapted it, prepared the prompt book, and then, like a latter-day Renaissance man, directed and produced it.

This bearing down on the humanities means a scanting of

other things. A girl who wants a mundane course in calculus or economics has to trot off to Pomona. Such a program also slips easily into extravagances.

Exam questions are sometimes amusing leaps of the imagination. One quiz opened with this piquant situation: "You find yourself in the company of the Canterbury pilgrims who, while riding, are discussing symbolism in art. . . ." Another question was steeped in a deep Spenglerian gloom: "You find yourself in heaven at a congress of historians debating whether or not Western civilization has defeated itself. . . ."

The Scrippsies are so imbued with passion for the timeless in literature that they scorn the contemporary (unless it is foreign). Only classics need apply even for informal dorm reading. The college librarian, exhausted by this intellectual mountain climbing, remarked tartly, "I sometimes wish they would join the Book-of-the-Month Club."

Scripps faculty, always first-rate, has been a kind of hatchery for college presidents. Pusey of Harvard, Jordan of Radcliffe, and Havens at Wilson all taught humanities there. There are no departments ("We meet in the corridors"), but faculty interchange is almost continuous. The humanities people meet regularly for discussion ("I got my liberal education at Scripps," a professor remarked). However, determined to escape the taint of the committee, they call their chairman a "convener." Each professor has his own private staff room—a delicious luxury which helps faculty amiability no end.

Scripps girls, like their Sarah Lawrence cousins, have the opportunity for a sustained I-thou dialogue with their professors. "Aren't you going to discuss Dante and the modern world?" a sweet young thing asked her humanities instructor. Forthwith they organized a talk session at his home, where, sprawled on the floor, they did a remorseless job of assigning each other to appropriate circles of hell.

Endless consorting with students can, of course, be wearing. At Christmas, a faculty member comes as Santa Claus and has to read student messages in verse—"Not quatrains but epics," he said grimly. The college runs a Spanish fiesta and barbecue. Getting into the spirit of things, one dignified classicist came as a Mexican cowboy, his unprepossessing shanks encased in tight pants. In the dressing room, he encountered another professor, equally outlandish in the garb of an Argentine ranch hand. "You know," he said sheeplishly, "I always did say you should read the small print in those damn college contracts."

As in any small family, there is a wry pleasure in local idiosyncrasies. Richard Armour, English professor and highly successful author of light verse and satire, is a push-up specialist. A lecturer who gets around the country, he once startled some genteel club ladies in the midst of a lecture by doing push-ups on the arms of a chair.

There are probably more visiting ceramicists debarking at Scripps than at any school in the country. (A guest potter declared sonorously, "T. S. Eliot says, 'Good prose cannot be written without convictions,' and I should like to add, 'nor good pots made either.' ") A girl held up a vase for my approval. "This is a hand-thrown pot right from the artsy-craftsy Scrippsy studio," she said with a twinkle.

I attended a rehearsal of *Jeremiah*, a stark modern dance composition. Leotard-clad girls moved, resolute and strong-thighed, across one of the lawns. The lead dancer was a natural—she had a gorgeous dancer's body and superb control, but with just a faint touch of Hollywood she wore dark sunglasses against the ubiquitous California sun.

In a discreet but stubborn way, Scrippsies want to marry. A few attend for two years, then shift to a university where the number of "eligibles" is larger. This would make of Scripps a kind of junior college—or, even worse, a finishing school. The faculty patiently explains that there is no natural break in college after two years, and has successfully kept most of its students.

Some return to school after marriage and even bring their children to lectures. One five-year-old, with imposing sangfroid, walked to the lectern after a learned discourse on Kant's *Critique of Pure Reason* and congratulated the professor on his performance.

Claremont Men's College (four hundred students and a faculty of forty) is lively and pleasantly brash. Militantly committed to free enterprise and "intelligent conservatism" (the adjective speaks volumes), it is no factory for NAM platitudes. It has an only partly tamed ex-Marxist on its faculty, and academic freedom is untrammeled. CMC is interested in the area where economics and government intersect and has therefore refurbished the archaic term "political economy." The school is designed to train leaders for business and government (and the less government the better!).

President George C. S. Benson argues that the United States has more political science teachers than the rest of the world combined, yet our political institutions are in sorry shape. He is vexed also by a curious distortion in higher education: by his estimate political science departments are 90 per cent Democratic in politics, economics departments 75 per cent. CMC, therefore, shops around for talented conservatives. "Benson," a professor explained reasonably, "is trying to redress the balance which now favors a soft, conformist liberalism. The school's ideology is a loose one: there is some connection between economic and political freedom; you cannot impair one without peril to the other."

"We're not a business administration school," Benson said testily. "The Scripps people haven't awakened to that fact yet. We have no professor of salesmanship or advertising. We do not belong to the Association of Collegiate Schools of Business. However, we do have economics majors, and we sharpen them up with tool subjects like accounting and statistics."

The quality of the students has picked up since 1947, when CMC began, and most of them currently come from the top quarter of their class. There is some congruence between the students and ethos of the college. Would-be tycoons, future Rotarians, CMC boys are exuberantly extroverted, tireless cheer leaders of fun, and—in their own self-image—mad, bad playboys. "Good dates," said one Scripps girl. "Idiots," said another. They are vociferously phallic, and the section on social life in their last yearbook was introduced by a photo of a handsomely constructed wench, barefoot and crinolined, landing rump-down on the ground.

Benson described them as ". . . free-enterprise types." There is a tangy individualism among them. Beards are not unknown among these students of high finance—nor bathing trunks in class. In a meeting I had with a group of students, the only one decorously dressed—in blue suit, white shirt, and tie—was the son of a trade-union official.

Their antics are legendary. Item: A Jaguar was found one morning straddling a small pool. Item: As a gag, the president of the sophomore class was shipped to Alaska. Item: *The Associated* reported matter-of-factly: "This semester's wienie-bake drew a fair-sized crowd, three police cars, two fire engines, and Dean Alamshah." Item: A youthful buccaneer in Honnold Library calmly took an electric shaver out if his attaché case, plugged it in, and began to shave. When he was sent on his way, he announced the date for an even bolder escapade. On the appointed date, before an immense audience, he pulled an electric iron out of his case, removed his pants, and began to iron them with impressive aplomb. (He was wearing bright red shorts.) Police were summoned, and in the ensuing commotion, the boy fled down the back stairs where he stumbled on the officers. "Go right up," he shouted. "There's a crazy guy loose up there who's ironing his pants." The story has a melancholy ending. He was put on conduct probation and became a good, gray citizen—even on Student Council.

CMC's program is rigorous: four years of humanities, senior thesis, and comprehensive exam, summer internship in government or industry. However, the grinds of Pomona are so odious to the CMC boys that they would prefer to disguise their intellectual status than be tarred with the image of the wimp. "We study in our closets," a CMC wag remarked.

President Benson spoke bluntly about academic standards: "CMC doesn't subsidize students; we attract them. We're now rejecting boys who would have been admitted to Pomona five years ago. We are in the top fifty or sixty colleges in the country admitting men—to judge by the College Board aptitude scores—but of course some students don't pan out."

Benson is admired by his faculty. And a visiting professor from another campus declared after talking with him: "My God! A college president who knows something."

The spontaneous flavor of CMC extends to the top. Dr. Benson was the only Claremont president to speak without restraint. He was even mildly fratricidal. Of Harvey Mudd College he said bluntly: "They bought their students—about 60 per cent are on scholarship." Of his own students he said; "Sure, there are always slobs in college. There are those who are unaffected by anything we do."

The danger in a new school is callowness, but CMC's staff consists of seasoned pros. The college has no beginning instructors, and as a result the faculty is more stable and mature than the average. In hiring faculty, CMC behaves with businesslike dispatch. "They made a direct offer fast," a professor recalled. "In other places, there's usually a lot of stalling on both sides."

The college makes a neat distinction between itself and the University of California. CMC's goal is that of the teacher-scholar; at Berkeley, it is the scholar-teacher. It believes that twenty young men well-taught are worth more than a minor research paper. On the other hand, a good teacher is expected to do some research—"solitary confinement at hard labor." But as one man said, "You don't worry about how many pounds you published this year." In any case, CMC has lured faculty away from such modish places as Harvard, Michigan, and Chicago.

Teaching at CMC is often an intellectual brawl. "The students," said Benson, "are basically conservative, but they get unsettled. Even when they're not bright, they give you a fight." Professors tease these paladins of free enterprise with Keynesian economics ("It kind of breaks them up a little"). But the faculty takes mundane pleasure in the success stories among alumni, some of whom are already heads of companies or big-time executives. A Pomona professor boasted about the Ph.D.'s his students would achieve. "But our students will hire them," a CMC teacher snapped.

How does an ex-Marxist fare in this Adam Smith dream country? An ex-Trotskyite with an incisive mind ("The Stalinists were too tepid for me") teaches political science at CMC.

"Why did Benson want me?" he mused. "He wasn't looking for a states' rights, laissez-faire man. That's a tawdry doctrine I hold in contempt. He really wanted a theorist, an avant-garde *Partisan Review* theorist. They read my doctoral thesis and decided I was more scholar than politico. But some of them are still waiting, because once you've been a socialist, you've got to be something."

He smiled with amusement. "They don't have me taped here," he said. "I'm not an ardent reactionary, like a lot of ex-radicals—not even a cool one. Then I'm not an ardent liberal either."

Teaching at CMC is not appreciably different from the University of Chicago, his former haven. "At Chicago," he recalled, "I had to be prudent and not violate liberal taboos—although I used to enjoy beating my students' heads in for their doctrinaire liberalism. Here I have to watch out for conservative taboos. But I'm beginning to feel free to smash some ikons.

"Lacking here are the two or three rare kids you find in every class in Chicago—those rare kids to whom you stretch out your hands to warm them. They work hard here; many are more literate than Chicago kids. The difference is that Chicago students are the sort who feel they have to hold an opinion about Marx or Freud. California kids have attitudes, not opinions, and attitudes don't have intellectual content."

The baby brother of the Associated Colleges is Harvey Mudd College of Science and Engineering. Under way in 1957, it now has one hundred and sixty students, including a few girls, and a faculty of twenty-seven. In 1960 it held its second commencement exercises for two lonely graduates (transfer students). Designed ultimately for three hundred and seventy-five students, the program at Harvey Mudd is geared to the needs of generalists in engineering or science rather than specialists. The college proceeds from the recognition that there is a new social dimension in the enormous power wielded by science. Formerly the question was, What *can* we do? Today it is, What *should* we do? Accordingly, one-third of the curricular time is devoted to the humanities and the social sciences. (Some students are seduced by the humanities and abandon science.) In graduate school Harvey Mudd products are likely to be a little ahead in science, a good deal ahead in the humanities, and slightly lagging in engineering.

The academic scrimmage at Harvey Mudd is bruising. Ten per cent of the first class, which was carefully selected, flunked out. The usual explanation is that California high schools, in the fell clutch of Life Adjustment, are too easy. At Harvey Mudd, classes are small, the tone intimate. "They have a distinguished faculty at Caltech," President Joseph Platt remarked, "but who teaches their freshman courses?"

Young as it is, the college has already spawned its student stereotype: precocious, addicted to hi-fi, home chemistry, and studies, unfrenzied socially. The students see themselves as "the slide-rule cowboys from the North Campus." In the boy-girl department, they do all right. "Most of the Scrippsies are thinking of marriage," a boy observed, "and an engineer or scientist these days is a gilt-edged security." Moreover, the emphasis on humanities at Harvey Mudd narrows the interest gap between them and the Scripps girls. A professor remarked, "Few are now intimidated by the Scripps girls, traditionally bluestockings, who two years ago seemed to our students to be intellectual snobs."

There is a good deal of excitement about getting a new college started. For one thing, it's no closet drama; lots of people—particularly the foundations—get in on the act. The faculty was given money to enable them to survey other programs before the college opened, and there was a six-week curriculum conference to which top-drawer educators from all over the country were invited. Two million words were recorded "to perpetuate our inconclusions." An authority on verbiage estimates that the Fund for the Advancement of Education got more words per dollar out of this grant than ever before. Some of these words were an indigestible farrago of pedagogy and engineering.

"Devising a curriculum is itself an engineering problem, involving definition of purpose, boundary conditions, and the optimization of the many possible solutions against an acceptable payoff function."

Far more attractive was a modest diary of the early days kept by Dr. George Wickes of Harvey Mudd's English Department. These are some entries:

September 26, 1957. After Chaplain Rankin had pronounced the benediction, we marched into the sun again, feeling a little solemn and a little gay, and altogether pleased that our college was now properly launched.

October 8. General alarm as Bill Davenport reported that some of our students are discouraged about their studies, a few to the point of being panic-stricken, one even ready to bolt. Probably they suffer only from a routine case of freshman blues, but without upperclassmen to diagnose their ailment, they are understandably demoralized.

December 2. We lost our first student today.

February 4, 1958. With so many non-smokers on the faculty, Gray has been offering lollipops in lieu of cigars. Too bad the Ford Foundation couldn't see us at faculty seminar this evening, sitting around in a circle sucking lollipops while dreaming up a scheme for the advancement of education.

The Associated Colleges are an upbeat academia. Robustly Californian, Claremont triumphs over problems which harass the rest of the country. The Group Plan adroitly combines the irresistible principle of growth in higher education with individuality. To the paleface Easterner, there is an overpowering impression of energy, money, and will. He hears talk in Claremont of a social science college for women, another coed school, and a school of creative writing. And in a startling but imaginative new plan, a Western outpost of Maryland's St. John's College will soon be established on the Claremont campus. But even in California, amid the fury of planning and building, basic questions about higher education remain finally unresolved. For whom? Toward what end?

SWARTHMORE: Use Thy Gumption!

Among the cognoscenti, Swarthmore College is one of the leaders of the academic procession. There are even those who commit the ultimate impiety of ranking the Quaker college above Harvard. A small school in a time of academic empires, Swarthmore is calmly impressive, for it starts with what most colleges strain to achieve: excellence.

The indices of Swarthmore's superiority are persuasive. In a study of the collegiate origins of scholars who attained the Ph.D. or other distinctions, Swarthmore ranked first for men and second for women in its productivity index. On the Medical College Admissions Test, Swarthmore students recently attained a dizzying 99th percentile—the highest possible ranking. The school's division of engineering—the country's smallest accredited engineering school—ranked seventh in the percentage of alumni in *Who's Who in Engineering*.

Swarthmore graduates contemplate a feast of abundance tendered by universities and foundations. The class of 1960 picked up a cool $85,000 in grants and fellowships, a goodly sum when one considers that there were only about one hundred students headed for graduate school. Fourteen won Woodrow Wilson Fellowships (honor-laden apprenticeships for college teaching), making Swarthmore Number One among small colleges. And even among the giants, this figure was equaled or exceeded by only eleven institutions. In that web of gossip that girdles academia, Swarthmore is pegged as one of the best schools in the country, with an unmatched capacity for inspiring academic passion in its students.

By virtue of its imposing credentials, the college is able to attract a freshman class of almost terrifying virtuosity. The 114 boys and 115 girls of the class of 1964 were culled from 2,263 avid applicants. Their College Entrance Examination Board scores showed a median score in the upper 600's. Among the freshmen there was a stunning array of academic and extracurricular talent: fifteen National Merit Scholarship winners, eight class presidents, seven student council presidents, twenty-five editors-in-chief of school publications, and, somewhat astonishingly, 101 varsity letter winners. (Swarthmore gives the lie to the wan stereotype of the bookish student. Her students—male and female—are athletes, hardy, and tireless.)

The college was established in 1864 by one branch of the Society of Friends, the Hicksites, who were bent on providing an education "equal to that of the best institutions of learning in the country." The founding fathers' philosophy has a contemporary ring: "What we Americans have most to fear is a dead level of mediocrity in the education of our people. Many persons seem to suppose that a moderate education, if joined with good common sense, is sufficient for all the purposes of life. It may be all that is needed for ordinary occasions, but not for the higher objects of our existence."

The school was originally housed in Parrish Hall, a huge, ungainly Victorian pile which is still the nerve center of the college, containing offices, dining rooms, and a women's dormitory. But there are now some forty-four buildings in all, including a new science building—all modern razzle-dazzle—and a recently opened women's dormitory, the usual cool tomb of glass and stone. The buildings run the gamut from lacy Gothic to the unrelievedly plain lines of a Friends Meeting House. The campus, a rural refuge of three hundred acres amid the encroachments of well-to-do suburbia (eleven miles southwest of Philadelphia) has a lovely sweep of meadow, blazes with color in the spring, and even has a stretch of honest-to-goodness woods.

Swarthmore has 960 students (500 men and 450 women) and 110 faculty members, which gives it a luxurious teacher-student ratio. The tone of the place is intimate, and faculty discussions are likely to turn on what "works" with a particular student.

The college is assiduously introspective. While Harvard has an impervious self-assurance, Swarthmore is in a constant fever of self-appraisal, for few schools have united such disparate elements. And it is the pull between its many polarities that gives the school its unique vivacity.

What is Swarthmore's personality? It is at once bookish yet high-spirited; Quaker yet mundane, with that heavy overlay of sophistication only the young can muster; inward yet careerist; bold yet conservative; bohemian yet fiercely social-minded. "What I like about this place," a girl said, "is that you can be listening to radicals one minute and be playing bridge the next."

There are two factors which give the college the effervescence and excitement that all visitors on campus quickly notice. ("I've never been so drained as I was at Swarthmore," a lecturer who gets around campuses remarked.) One is simply the sheer concentration of brainy kids. Harvard conveys the same sense of intellectual plenty—an untamed precocity which is almost comic when it is not intimidating. But Harvard boys take fewer chances intellectually. Swarthmore students have far more warmth and color—and recklessness. (It is partly the bohemian sanction of adventuring with intellect, partly the Quaker tradition of the inner light and individual conscience.) The second factor is the Quaker tolerance of diversity. There is no unifying ethos at Swarthmore—except that the life of the mind is good—and one can find warring camps in a state of highly vocal coexistence.

The most celebrated split is that which separates fraternity men (and their feminine satellites) and the Bohemians, whose Holy City, the Mary Lyon dormitory for men, is now being abandoned. Swarthmoreans (in facetious moments they call themselves Swarthmorons) make dramatic capital out of this schism; it gives them a sense of plenitude. Freshmen like to think that they have to make an ideological choice between the gay insipidity of fraternity life and black-garbed dissidence. The lines are rigidly drawn, at least in theory. Fraternity men are likely to be athletic, conservative politically, impeccably white-shoe—solid if tame citizens of Philistia. ("How many regular guys are there at Swarthmore?" a townie asked a football player. "About thirty," he answered forlornly.) The Bohemian males are, reputedly, disheveled, bearded and sandaled, given to intellectual and artistic pursuits, addicted to folk music and green book bags, and chronically intransigent.

But there are complex modulations to this neat scheme. At exam time fraternity men are prone to let their beards grow. And a fondness for folk music is part of the Swarthmore life style (although the Greeks are likely to indulge furtively). And fraternity men, with the local receptivity to ideas, will on occasion invite a Bohemian to talk to them about "Individuality and the Dangers of Fraternity Life." On the other side of the barricades, the Bohemian-artistic group shows a most uncharacteristic athletic flair. And one of the deans remarked, "The kids in blue jeans and beards who call themselves Bohemian will read to the blind in Overbrook or run programs at Norristown Mental Hospital."

Swarthmore students cherish the deep fissure in their collective psyche, and there is some uneasiness that the vigorous dialectic of the past may be abated by a mushy consensus psychology. A girl said elegiacally: "People are always talking about the giants of the past—those who went barefoot or were magnificently amoral. Now everyone is crew-cut and normal and boring. Every year when the freshmen enter, the upperclassmen look them over and say, 'What dull clods!' "

A graduate looked back nostalgically at the school's heroic days (only three or four years distant): "Those were the days when there were fraternity men on one side, and the others on the other side, and you knew what you stood for. These days there are a lot of vociferous neutrals who botch up the ideological lines."

"The only giants," a cold-eyed student said wryly after listening to a recital of past glories, "are those who keep talking about how there *were* giants."

President Courtney Smith locates the center of Swarthmore's personality in the clashing of ideas and interest groups, in an intimacy which results not in accommodation but in a lively confrontation.

"There's a myth," he said, "that if you have two sons and one is big and gregarious, you send him to Yale or Princeton or Harvard to meet the ultimate challenge. If the other is shy and introspective, you send him to a small college like Swarthmore. But that's a mistake. At Harvard you find your interest group—it could be Arabic or chess—and you stay with it. You're sealed off from other groups. At Swarthmore, precisely because it is small and intimate, you have to defend your interest against many others."

There is a beguiling touch of the zany about Swarthmore. An engineering student bought a hearse for use by the Engineers Club—and for the best reasons, he argued cogently: not only is its carrying capacity superior to that of most cars, but also its motor was not abused in dolorous journey between funeral parlor and cemetery. In a philosophy class I saw a boy pass his pipe to a pretty girl, a combed-hair type, who puffed reflectively a few times, then passed it back. Up front, the professor lectured on the mind-body problem. And some years ago, a huge sign announcing "Almonzo is pinned" was painted on the water tower, 118 feet above the campus, to warn the unwary about a philandering student who was going steady.

"Use thy gumption," a Quaker professor of mathematics used to urge her students. And Swarthmore students do, often with extraordinary results. But there is another key phrase which epitomizes the college: "return to order." And it is this conviction about the requirements of group living that tempers the excesses to which Swarthmore students are prone. Between these two poles, the spirit of the institution can be found.

The Quaker spirit is subtly pervasive, but its influence is difficult to appraise. (About 15 per cent of the students come from Quaker families.) The tendency to hold authority to a minimum (even if students say the minimum is too high), an inclination to think well of people, and an old-fashioned inner-directed character—all of these may be Quaker in origin. Certainly, the honor paid to kitchen and custodial employees upon their retirement—announced in the same fashion as the retirement of professors—attests to a die-hard Quaker simplicity. And though the "thee's" and "thou's" of an earlier era have vanished, there are still traces of Quaker idiom in First Day (Sunday) and Collection (chapel).

I attended a Quaker Meeting on campus, which is not, by the way, an official College activity. Though the usual opportunities were provided for the expression of the "inner light," those in attendance were too well bred for its spontaneous assertion. Instead there was a kind of *structured inner light*. After a long silence, one woman got up and talked about a visit to a home for unwed mothers with a curious mixture of Quaker piety and sociological jargon.

There is a strong centripetal pull on campus. The college is an intense, self-isolating little cosmos. Students rarely go to Philadelphia, only a half-hour away, and the homing instinct is abetted by an all-purpose student fee which procures admission to every event on campus. The residents of Swarthmore—it is called The Ville—and the college community view each other with remote and polite distrust. *The Phoenix*, the student newspaper, describes the town as "the real world," where "police can be friendly." Perhaps they take their cue for cautious disdain from former President Aydelotte who characterized Swarthmore as "a town of contented dogs and happy children." The students are affronted by the suburb's homogeneity (few Jews and Negroes) and by its Organization Man blandness. They are sometimes taunted by local children with the name "Turkey" (bookworm), or are asked by adults, "Is it true you have absolutely no standards of dress?" To many *villeniks* the college reeks vaguely of socialism and unbridled sex, although there is also a grudging admiration for the school's top-heavy intellectualism. It is possible, too, that the students, contemplating this trim upper-class town, bristle at the image of suburban *Gleichschaltung* (cultural coordination) which awaits them.

The college administration watches the town-gown relationship morosely. ("One of the primary aims of the College," *The Phoenix* quipped, "is to keep the Village happy.") A dean described his relief when Williams College students visited and townspeople saw that they too were bearded.

The administration has its headaches. The official philosophy is that "it values values." Given hundreds of intense young people, their values, sometimes flamboyantly proclaimed and practiced, can be an administrative nuisance. The same is true of the school's philosophy of individualism. In the abstract, a joy; in reality, individualism can be nettlesome, especially in a conservative community. (Swarthmore has been described as radical in ideas and conservative in social behavior—the latter, assertedly, is the price one pays for the former.)

The upshot of all this is an unremitting contest between students and administration, the students complaining of being policed too much, and college officials reluctant to bring into play the apparatus of authority so vulgarly applied elsewhere. There is also constant soul-searching by everyone about the tricky line of demarcation between freedom and license.

To the outsider the tone of the college seems briskly libertarian. Swarthmore was one of the first schools to repudiate the disclaimer affidavit in the National Defense Education Act and to disengage from the benefits of that program. The appearance on campus of an Assistant Secretary of the Air Force to discuss modern weaponry inspired a letter to the school newspaper protesting his appearance in the light of the Quaker tradition. He gave his talk but so have Linus Pauling, Harry Bridges, and other representatives of dissenting groups. The college jealously protects freedom of inquiry, and it is perhaps a modest enough qualification when President Smith asserts: "This freedom can best be defended if the invitations to speakers are thoughtfully issued, and if students are aware of the variety of opinions already scheduled to be heard."

Swarthmore's most imposing quality is its unmodulated academic zeal. The administration can intone grandiosely about the goal of the well-rounded student (well-rounded *on a high level*, it is quick to add), but the truth is that Swarthmore is simple-mindedly and gloriously bookish. The impassioned academic life is what attracts students and also kills them off. (The drop-out rate is a high 25 per cent as against Harvard's 10 per cent. And drop-outs are largely academic, for even the professionally malcontent love Swarthmore, and the school sometimes has trouble keeping them away when they have officially severed their relationship.) "Ours is one of those offbeat colleges," a senior observed, "where someone when asked how he spends his free time may answer in all honesty, 'I study.'" Another senior recalled a relentless four-year dialogue with a philosophy professor on ontological proof "with each of us reversing his position at least twice." And there is the apocryphal story of the visitor who came for a Saturday afternoon football game and dutifully followed a thick stream of students—right into the library!

More than half of Swarthmore's girls go on to graduate study —a far higher percentage than at most of the good women's colleges. Unlike women at many other schools, the girls are not prone to play down their intellectual talents for fear of pricing themselves out of the marriage market. At Swarthmore the men and women are intellectual peers—even loving combatants. During the first two years, the girls actually get higher grades, but their performance declines somewhat during their last two years when the marriage pressure becomes grim.

At Freshman Serenade, male and female act out symbolically their intellectual tug-of-war. First, the girls fulfill the formal motif of the occasion by singing a few songs—even then they usurp the masculine role. Thereupon, the boys douse them savagely with water and roll them downhill. The girls emerge as muddy harridans.

Academic arrangements are a blend of the advanced and conservative. Swarthmore's honors program was one of the pacesetters of progressive education almost four decades ago. On the other hand, it is ironic that a school which is so robustly socialminded and international—no crisis is too remote for the students' sympathy or indignation—should lack sociology and anthropology departments. Moreover, not a single painting or short story is done as part of course work. (The campus jumps with creativity, but it is extracurricular.) Then there are odd interstices in the curriculum. Swarthmore never got on the great books or humanities bandwagon, and one student was dismayed to discover that in no course on campus was it possible to study Dante.

A spokesman for the college had a ready explanation for their stand-pat attitude. "A lot of the experimentation going on elsewhere," he argued, "is fake. It's just an expression of nervousness. There are colleges that think they have failed if they don't get a box in the education page of the Sunday *Times*."

Swarthmore students and faculty take pleasure, not unmixed with pain, in their strenuous academicism. A classics professor who taught at Columbia related how if he failed to give an assignment at the school in New York his students, quietly exultant, would fail to remind him. At Swarthmore, they would be sure to prod him.

"It's highly competitive," a student said. "Nobody asks what you got on an exam, but it's there just the same. The academic atmosphere is what I like, but I don't like being pushed or dragged. Even on vacation, students will work six or eight hours a day."

"I was an A student in high school," a boy said dolefully. "I came here and worked twice as hard but wound up with a C average."

Campus heroes are not merely the A-producing mind-machines, but those handy with ideas. A fatal dispersion of energy can result, perhaps best exemplified by a pretty girl who said, "I've been trying to study for a physics exam all week, but I've been preoccupied with a philosophic problem."

A Radcliffe girl who visited Swarthmore summed up the difference between the two schools: "At Swarthmore I get the feeling that a student is encouraged to believe that his ideas have significance. At Radcliffe you feel that everything has been said and that you're hopelessly naive."

All this intellectual hustle and bustle begets a characteristically mocking reaction. A sign on a Parrish Hall bulletin board magisterially announced the formation of the Peripheral Information Society for the advancement of non-specialized knowledge—the first speaker, Hubris Johnson, an authority on such things as the average height of mango trees.

Adventuring with ideas receives its loftiest apotheosis in Swarthmore's celebrated honors program. Back in the twenties, the college, under the leadership of Frank Aydelotte, pioneered in independent study to defeat what he called "the academic lockstep." The rest of academia took more than three decades to catch on.

About 40 per cent of Swarthmore's upperclassmen take honors. Instead of the usual four courses carried by juniors and seniors, an honors student carries two seminars each semester during his junior and senior years. The eight seminars he will carry, in no more than three fields, are expected to fall into a coherent academic pattern—in effect, comprising a major field and two minor fields (e.g., literature, philosophy, history). The rationale of the program is that instead of the usual transmission of knowledge from teacher to student, the young scholar should work on his own in areas that have intellectual urgency for him, should achieve some depth and sophistication in those areas, and should share his experiences with a small community of scholars.

Each seminar meets once a week often in the professor's home for a session of at least three hours. The groups are small—usually under half a dozen students—and though some seminars do assign readings, the core of the process is the discussion of papers prepared by students. These are subjected to merciless appraisal, which goes on and on long past the allotted three hours. The only break is provided by the faculty wife who, at one point in the proceedings, pacifies the gladiators with coffee and cake.

This is an authentic community of scholars, since not even examinations—that ugly trauma that separates professor from student—disturb its unity. At the end of his senior year, the honors student takes eight 3-hour written exams prepared by outside examiners. ("Discuss convention in Renaissance poetry. . . . Whenever we put two emotions in juxtaposition, we have what we can properly call an idea. Illustrate from several poems by Donne. . . .") The examiners turn up later for a follow-up oral quiz. (They are often so impressed by Swarthmore's intellectual muscle that they wind up sending their own children there.) The student and his professor, therefore, are intellectual partners who make common cause against the outside examiner.

Dr. Daniel Hoffman, a gifted poet and scholar, acknowledged that many of his ideas come out of seminar discussions. "That's just fine," President Smith commented. "He puts ideas into the seminar and takes other ideas out."

The honors program has its critics. A former Swarthmore student, now a professor elsewhere, asked testily, "Is it better to have a group of students talk about something they know very little about than to have a structured lecture by a professor who does?" There are those who object to the cult of Aydelotte ("Aydelotte was God, and we are his prophets"). Others complain, with mutually canceling logic, that the seminars are too well organized and thus differ little from course work, or too flexible and discursive. To guard against intellectual chaos, the college not long ago instituted a general education program during the first two years to assure common learning.

There are groans about the exams at the end of senior year—"two years work in ten days . . . terror and breakdown!" A professor took a lighter view: "It's the big sporting event of the year; we make book on the results." One of its more entertaining if cruel features is that anyone may watch the oral interrogation. Certainly the honors program is a rousing intellectual Olympiad for most students. And the experience of a girl, while doing graduate work in journalism, was revealing. Asked to do a practice piece on a UN committee she researched seventeenth-century precursors of international cooperation so exhaustively that her professor was provoked to say, "Fine, but are you writing for the man in the subway or for the faculty of Swarthmore College?" No remark could have pleased her more.

In a spirit at once respectful and skeptical, I attended a few seminars. There were amusing touches in a seminar in Modern European Literature. Sitting on a couch were two girls with unkempt hair, bobby socks—and flawless manners. A male student, resplendently bearded, was wearing a tie and jacket (mandatory dress for seminars) and also army combat boots. The professor opened the discussion with the question, "By what means does Dostoevski implement his non-conceptual communication in *The Brothers Karamazov?*" The verbiage flew—some of it mere verbal bloat, some of it beautifully disciplined and formulated. There were even epigrammatic flourishes. One boy described Smerdyakov as "a kind of diseased limb." "Yes," his professor answered, "he is the degeneration of the life-affirming impulse."

At one point, the professor, gently reproachful, corrected a seminar paper. "You seem to have a preference," he said to a young man, "for spelling *existence* with an *a.* It's commonly spelled with an *e,* I believe." In the kitchen, the professor's wife was rattling the coffee cups, in preparation for the break, while her husband was saying, "We live in a timeless dimension in this book. . . ."

In a philosophy seminar this problem was under discussion:

"Why does the fact that we seem to remember anything pre-suppose that there is such a thing as memory?" In the midst of a tortuous formulation, an ungainly dog pushed open the door with his nose and shambled amiably across the room. The pro-fessor immediately translated this event into cautious philosophic language: "A canine patch recently seemed to proceed across the room." The students laughed but proceeded to examine the proposition while the dog, his head on his paws, listened drowsily. Present at the seminar was another professor of philosophy who, though on leave, is unable to resist the weekly tourney of minds.

At a modern poetry seminar T. S. Eliot's esotericism was eso-terically analyzed. ("What I meant by the third level of mean-ing . . ." a student began.) The seminar papers ranged from inept imitations of *The Sewanee Review* to highly perceptive textual analyses. Along with solid scholarly work, there were the usual sins of precocity—overingenious formulations, shrill ped-antry, and turgidity of style. There is even an established critical parlance comprising such words as *undercut, qualify, ironic,* etc. (One virtuoso of seminarsmanship recently wrote an all-purpose seminar paper in which one merely has to fill in the blanks with the specific matter of the subject.)

In the poetry seminar, Professor Daniel Hoffman, with a poet's eye for imagistic precision, criticized a line that included "an offshoot that is geared . . ." The student bristled. "That is my diction," he muttered politely. "That's all very well," Hoffman countered, affable, *and* firm, "but it's untenable."

If Swarthmore students are ardent about things most college students are indifferent to—the world of ideas—they also seem to make a point of their indifference to social life, the vital center in the lives of most college students. There are certain antistereotype stereotypes on campus. A Saturday night date, for example, is not de rigueur, and students will casually get together at Somerville, the snack bar, and pick up companions for a movie. Nor are there restrictions with respect to class and age. A senior girl loses no status by going out with a suitable freshman boy. They are all citizens in good standing in the Republic of Letters.

There is simply less social fervor at Swarthmore than in most schools. There are the usual dances, but as a student summed up,

"Some people think they're fun; others go ironically, and then there are those who won't even get out of their sneakers."

"The girls subside into neuterness," a boy said sulkily. "When you go down to breakfast and see the grimy people and grimy eggs, you get discouraged."

Nevertheless, spring comes as explosively to Swarthmore as anywhere else. "In the springtime," a girl said, "there's the great domestic idyll—couples cemented together. They're in every tree."

But lovers must run an obstacle course hand in hand. Cars are outlawed on campus except for use by organizations. Visiting in the dorms is limited to Sunday afternoon—"it's less immoral during the day," a boy said—with the door open six inches. ("How many sections of the *Times* does that require?" a student asked.) And a watchful eye must be kept open for proctors, the student constabulary—"paid agents with dirty minds" in the phrase of one critic.

Then there are the Lodges, social rooms in what used to be sorority houses before sororities voted themselves out of existence. Students, even couples, may reserve these rooms for a few hours to prepare a meal or study over a cup of coffee.

Marriage on campus is virtually proscribed. The college insists that one of the marrying parties must leave school—unless they are both over twenty-one, have their parents' consent, and are exceedingly good students. For amorous dalliance, therefore, this leaves only a few possibilities: climbing into dorms—a perilous business in defiance of college regulations—or, weather permitting, Crum Woods, the source of a rich romantic folklore.

Crum Woods has been humorously elevated into a branch of the curriculum—the Department of Applied Erotics—and celebrated in verse:

> Crum Woods is the coed's doom
> Evening shadows fill the gloom
> Suddenly there comes a hush
> The dean is checking underbrush.

Former Dean Hunt used to see students in each other's arms on the lawn in front of the library. A popular, avuncular figure, he would chide them gently and ask, "Why don't you go into Crum Woods?" "That would be hypocritical," a moral stalwart answered.

In the cold of winter, I saw one couple, evidently in despair of finding privacy, standing nose to nose in silent intensity in the middle of an enormous room in Somerville. Nevertheless, despite the grim handicaps, Swarthmore has somehow earned the name of "the Little Quaker Matchbox."

One of the issues separating fraternity men and Bohemians concerns the opportunities for privacy in fraternity houses—often called "[little] dens of immunity." This is hotly denied by both fraternity men and the administration. However, when I visited a fraternity house one afternoon, under a photograph in full color of Miss Playmate of the Month (the tutelary saint?), a couple hastily disengaged themselves from an embrace as we entered.

The dialectic between fraternity men and Bohemians has other nodal points. Frat boys were described by one girl as "more the oglers and scorekeepers." Bohemians, Greeks counter, smell bad— "popular mythology without empirical basis," a bearded young man said. "We just go out of our way," he added, "*not to go out of our way* to look nice."

But despite the *Kulturkampf*, fraternities have a distinctly Swarthmorean cast. Discrimination is far less flagrant than elsewhere—one of the five fraternities has already disaffiliated nationally—and the hazing is free from sadism. "It's stylish to criticize fraternities," a boy remarked. And some young men even join with reformist intent: they hope to make the fraternities go local or even liquidate themselves.

In any case, fraternity men and bohemians—and those who rally around no ideological banner—meet amiably on the playing fields of Swarthmore. For a school so enchanted with intellect, it is astonishingly athletic. Fifty-five per cent of its male students participate in eleven intercollegiate sports, and the school fields able, if aseptically amateur, teams, including a football team— small-time stuff, to be sure.

Football is not king at Swarthmore. Soccer and cross-country seem to arouse a distinctively Swarthmorean ardor—soccer because of its technical refinements (football is brutish by comparison), and cross-country because it attracts intellectuals.

The affinity for sports may reflect the influence of Cecil Rhodes, who demanded "physical vigor" and "a fondness for manly sports" in his scholarship winners. (The headquarters for the Rhodes Scholarships are located at Swarthmore.) And the girls, too, show the same affinity for locker room and sweatshirt, with 35 per cent of them on teams. For reasons hard to fathom, they are invincible swimmers and have won countless meets.

The Big Day is when the soccer and football teams both play Haverford, the traditional rival, as part of the competition for the Hood Trophy. The effort to stir the school to fighting pitch has comic overtones. A pep rally marched on the library to rouse the sluggish only to be doused with water by a subversive in the library tower. And freshman zealotry, expressed in fierce slogans like "Kill Haverford" and "Emulsify our Rivals," was countered by posters counseling peace ("Love Thy Neighbor") and by an ironic sketch of the Madonna saying, "Go and kill Haverford, my son." And it is perhaps only at Swarthmore that a rah-rah sign would be couched in the nonhortatory idiom of syllogism: "School spirit equals football spirit. Therefore, school equals football."

The campus a few years ago was mildly shaken by a conflict between a crack soccer player with a bushy beard, of which he was inordinately fond, and his coach. The latter demanded that he get rid of his beard or leave the team. He finally resigned from the team to the cheers of friends who saw an important principle at stake. (One dissenter said lugubriously, "We'd have won all the games too!") A history professor, another bearded one, wrote a letter to *The Phoenix* affirming his solidarity with the soccer player.

By all accounts, the faculty at Swarthmore is superb. At a time when faculty raiding is the big sport of academia and universities dangle fancy laboratories and gifted graduate students under the twitching nostrils of professors, how does Swarthmore keep its best people? One answer is that Swarthmore has jacked up its salaries—about 67 per cent since 1954. Salaries now range from

$5,400 to $17,000; with the average for assistant professors, $7,500; associate professors, $9,600; and full professors, $12,700. Fringe benefits are enticing: leave as often as every four years, either a half year at full pay, or a full year at half pay. The teaching load is nine hours a week and twelve hours in the sciences—no cinch for a conscientious teacher but not crushing either.

Although academic excellence is a condition of employment, the yardstick of publication is not applied coarsely at Swarthmore. "Large universities because of their size and impersonality can't evaluate their faculty except by counting bibliographical items," a college spokesman explained. "It makes professors run out to get quick results. We don't have to do that here." They do publish, however, in reputable scholarly journals, and the research that goes on takes place virtually in the students' laps.

But the principal attraction is an intellectually bracing atmosphere. "It's a happy cycle," Smith pointed out, "strong students draw strong faculty, who, in turn, draw strong students." A faculty wife said with quiet assurance, "We are house-proud here."

Faculty conferences are a lively blend of Roberts Rule of Order and Quaker Meeting. If a vote is close, the discussion continues until greater harmony is attained. At other colleges, a dean recalled, when there is an academic procession you fall into line in accordance with rank and date and appointment. ("It could be heart-searing to be in the back.") At Swarthmore one just falls in line anywhere. "If there are young Turks on the faculty," a youthful professor said, "it's merely on procedural matters."

To be sure, the college is no dovecote, and it has its lively contretemps. On a picturesque level, there was resentment when a professor, the owner of what is virtually a baronial estate, asked his less affluent neighbors to remove laundry from their clotheslines on the eve of a cocktail party he was giving. On a more serious level, a teacher of literature expressed dismay about a few science professors who failed to oppose the disclaimer affidavit. "Some of them sound as if they haven't read a newspaper in ten years," he said indignantly.

A gifted young professor, who was not given tenure and has moved on, expressed a harsh minority view. "There is an Establishment here," he said truculently. "What counts is family, manners, chic—knowing which books are discussed in the literary supplement of the London *Times*. There is a measure of arrogance and self-satisfaction here that can be infuriating. Swarthmore isn't the only college that really means A when it bestows one."

The college did not keep one of its most scintillating professors, described by *The Phoenix* in *Partisan Review* fashion as "a charismatic culture hero." Nimble in disputation and shatteringly handsome, this philosophy professor is implausibly, a kind of modern Renaissance man interested in the philosophy of science, car design, psychoanalysis, and—with an engaging touch of the bizarre—psychic phenomena. A swashbuckler behind the wheel, he was constantly barreling around campus in one rakish sports car after another or in his celebrated white Cadillac. For a pet, he kept an obscure, sharp-toothed tropical rodent. An articulate spokesman for dissenting views, he was described by one student as "the new God in the Pantheon since he dethroned the old Gods." This may be a case of life imitating legend too faithfully. He was so richly in the Swarthmore grain—so venturesome, buoyant, and intellectually uncompromising—that in the end he could only end up as a kind of faculty gadfly.

There are those who argue that the admissions policy is unsound. The children of alumni (10 per cent of the student body) allegedly drag down the academic level. (They tend to do a little below average.) These critics assert that talk about "a balanced community" is merely a device for circumventing a purely intellectual measure of admission—the only one that should prevail. One professor derogated the "sentimental extravagance" of the personal interview. "We've had remarks like 'He's a fine American boy,'" he said. "Hell, we don't care about that. We want to know if he can work—not if he has a crew-cut."

Swarthmore likes to see its deans as "amateur administrators," with one foot firmly planted in the classroom. In comparison with the ponderous administrative apparatus elsewhere, Swarthmore has a right to this genial image. (It has no department of personnel service with its pseudoscientific jargon about pupil-personnel problems, counseling is rather informal, and the deans are people who read books.) Moreover, there is no dean of faculty, on the grounds that professors need no buffer between the president and themselves. But amateurs or no, the administrators have their share of alarums and excursions, for the campus buzzes with issues and the students are quick to indignation.

Dr. Courtney Smith, Swarthmore's able president since 1953, has had a productive tenure. A former Rhodes Scholar from Harvard and an English professor at Princeton, Smith has raised salaries, built up endowment, and energetically maintained the college's tradition of excellence. He has many admirers, although he has had to live down the inevitable stereotype of the Madison Avenue executive. He is good-looking, youthful, crew-cut, and has a cool, unblinking composure. (Intensity is more in the Swarthmore style.) One professor suggested that Smith has been, on balance, "a force for conservatism," another argued that the new faculty prosperity had elements in it of "a demeaning paternalism," but most felt that he has been vigorous and successful with a sound instinct for giving his professors lots of autonomy.

Student life at Swarthmore is vivid, mercurial, and hectic. Even when they deplore their apathy, Swarthmore students do so with great verve. They are ferociously interested in everything that takes place on campus and off, and nowhere are students so profligate with language. They write polemics on a variety of issues and stick them on the bulletin boards, or they tack up manifestos in firm expectation that someone will rise to the challenge. (And someone always does. These exchanges can go on for weeks—with marginal notations by intellectual kibitzers.) "We're so intimate here, it's positively incestuous," the son of a college president remarked. *The Phoenix* has little of the icy disdain or imperturbability of the Harvard *Crimson*, but it is immensely entertaining, often stormy, and sometimes howlingly funny. And nowhere in the country do students write such long, erudite, and doggedly argumentative letters to the editor. Swarthmore students care—and care deeply.

What is it they care about? There are first the public issues—nuclear policy, sit-in demonstrations, and civil rights—that have recently shaken American youth from the mindless grip of the drowsy fifties. Swarthmore students have been in the vanguard of all these movements. A busload of students participated in the Youth March for Integration, another group attended Congressional committee hearings on the Vienna Youth Festival, and students picketed Woolworth's during the sit-in demonstrations in the South. Locally, a student committee sat with Negro families during the troubled time when they moved into an all-white suburban community. And one mettlesome girl on a visit to Cuba, marched right into the headquarters of the secret police, who proudly showed her how clean the cells were.

But political action these days involves far more than bare-knuckled idealism; it has, in fact, a markedly sophisticated flavor. Many Swarthmore students are not satisfied with the mere thrust and shove of student demonstrations. Well-schooled in the dynamics of power, operators as well as visionaries, they lean towards the expedient and the politic. Picketing Woolworth's was followed by a meeting to discuss its efficacy. A student leader dismissed the March for Integration as "merely inflammatory," and explained his strategy of applying pressure at sensitive points. As a symbol of the new political sophistication, Swarthmore is the headquarters of *Albatross*, an intercollegiate magazine which will publish copies of political letters written by students and professors to men in public life. These letters thus are transformed into powerful social instruments, which public officials can ignore only at their own peril.

Local affairs provoke rough-and-tumble discussion. The fraternity men and the anti's belabor each other periodically. There is disgruntlement about mandatory attendance at Collection, and there are self-styled conscientious objectors. *The Phoenix*, in irreverent spirit, took a poll on how students feel about Collection. Suggestions for improvement included program lights on back of seats to read by; stamp machines and mailboxes at the exits; and a fall seminar for freshmen on rustle-proof page turning. Even the jukebox at the Somerville snack bar provokes Socratic dialogues. Recently, a petition protesting rock 'n' roll was pasted on the jukebox, with a counterpetition right under it which insisted that rock 'n' roll is authentic folk music.

A far grimmer issue is that perennial college headache: dining-room fare. A day-long food strike united even those chronic belligerents, the Bohemians and the Greeks. (A girl described the dining room as the "sordid center" of the college. "The food is so blah," she explained, "that it makes the people around you seem blah. It becomes a mark of sensitivity to cringe when you stand in the dining room line.")

A perfervid discussion was unleashed when President Smith, in a Collection talk, urged the students to dress more attractively. (An earlier effort to get students to wear appropriate shoes to the dining room backfired. In protest, a group marched barefoot to the dining room.) "Smith wants to create a kind of Quaker Princeton," a boy said. In any event, the columns of *The Phoenix* churned for weeks thereafter with students affirming and rejecting but always probing, analyzing, defining. Would conservative habits of dress change the character of the school? Is it necessary to dress restrainedly to make one's advanced political ideas prevail? Is dress connected with the artist's search for absolute beauty? Is it true that the "great unfettered of the past" have not objected to social conformity? And so on through the night and down the word-engorged columns of *The Phoenix.* Entirely characteristic was an article on fall fashions at Swarthmore a few years ago, featuring photos of a nubile maiden, which defined the sartorial pieties: "That well-worn look is seen everywhere, especially in the faded denim of the blue jean, an absolute must for your college wardrobe. For wear atop the blue jean, we hear that the sweatshirt is in this year as always . . . in classic gray cozily lined with lint. Nothing is quite so chic as the tennis shoe also known as the sneaker. And a new look on the Swarthmore scene this year is the work shirt. . . ."

Another minor crisis was occasioned by the annual Folk Festival (folk singing by professionals and amateurs and folk dancing). The high capital of the folk mystique, Swarthmore each spring is visited by guitar-thumping collegians from distant points, many of whom used to sleep in Crum Woods. The folk festival was discreetly changed to a one-day affair with the usual breast-beating by students that Swarthmore's great days are over.

A somber note was struck by a spate of recent editorials in *The Phoenix* expressing horror at a number of thefts at the school. An alumna recalled an episode at a bar in a nearby town, when her companion, a Swarthmore student, deliberately picked up the hat of an innocent man standing nearby. Another drinking companion then emptied out his pockets and proudly displayed six ashtrays which had been deftly appropriated.

"There's a kind of innocent amorality about some of the students," she explained. "They're so bright, they feel they can achieve anything, do anything. You take kids who were unpopular at high school because of their intellectualism, and you put them in an atmosphere in which they're at home, and this is what can happen. Then when they get out into the world, they have to get used to restraints again."

But these unfortunate tendencies have to be measured against the immense social usefulness of most students, the stern morality of the college's conscientious objectors, or the young couple seriously determined to create a utopian colony in British Columbia.

The visitor to Swarthmore is impressed most of all by the unexpected gaiety and ebullience of the intellectual life as practiced at Swarthmore. Whether they are boning up in the library or engaged in such local sports as penny-pitching or sliding down the library walk on metal trays in winter, the students do so with characteristic zest and with a full play of intelligence. Everything is grist—playfully or seriously—for the intellectual mill, whether it's Frisbee ("the Frisbee aesthetic is not one of guttural snarlings . . . the true zealot aims for the aura of classic repose"), the fraternity issue, or even a visit to a burlesque show ("the dance moved through various stages of canonic treatment leading to a fortissimo climax"). And it is symbolically appropriate, in this vortex of individualism, that IBM machines, introduced a few years ago, did not prove to be feasible.

A profoundly revealing remark was made by a professor who was not given tenure. He was angry, unappeasably angry, and he fulminated against the college, its policies, and its arrogant faculty. Suddenly, he stopped and said quietly, "Of course, when I criticize, I do so from way up here." And he reached up with his right arm as high as he could. "And the reason I'm so angry, I guess," he went on, "is that Swarthmore is a scholar's Eden, and here I am banished!"

Colleges with a Local Flavor

BROOKLYN COLLEGE:
Culture in Flatbush

About three miles from ghost-haunted Ebbets Field, Brooklyn College sits on what alumnus Irwin Shaw has called "the melancholy plain of Flatbush." An area whose lonely vistas appalled Thomas Wolfe ("Only the dead know Brooklyn," he intoned), it is, in truth, a robustly middle-class area full of neat one- and two-family homes, which made it in its time a precursor of Suburbia. Urban blight has not overtaken Flatbush, and the college is an island of learning awash with domesticity. Its greensward is as likely to be patrolled by local mothers clutching babies as by students with texts under their arms. The huge Georgian buildings are just around the corner from a major shopping area, and it is only in the immediate environs of the college that a campus character wanly asserts itself—bookstores and eating places and a recently opened Ivy League men's shop as a symbol of a new sophistication.

Brooklyn College is distinctive in a number of ways. For the record, it is a college, but in size—17,000 liberal arts students and a staff of almost a thousand—it is equal to a state university. It is a free college, with some heartening things to tell us about subsidized higher education at a time when we are nervous about what the Russians are doing in higher education. It is nondenominational—a lofty high-school average is the only ticket of admission —but, because of Brooklyn's population make-up, it is 85 per cent Jewish and has only a handful of America's dominant group, white Anglo-Saxon Protestants. It has more Jewish students than any collegiate institution in Israel or, for that matter, than Yeshiva University. Because Brooklyn College crackles with learning from

83

early morning until late at night, it is possibly the most over-worked physical plant in the country (though beautifully main-tained), and large-scale repairs have to wait until August when an unnatural calm descends on the campus. (There is a brief and graceful hiatus daily around 6 P.M. when the last of the day stu-dents have trudged home, alive with the triumphs and outrages of the last class, and the evening students, with their impassive business faces, have not yet arrived.)

Brooklyn College is a subway school, as its students will plain-tively tell you. As a reminder of the city's bountifulness, it is directly across the street from Midwood High School, whose archi-tectural scheme harmonizes with that of the college. For many of the college's students, there are no rites of passage. They are graduated from Midwood High School and simply cross the nar-row street to the college. This, they point out, is hardly a change. That the college operates on a kind of double session (morning and afternoon schedules) only intensifies the sense of not having moved beyond the ambiance of high school.

Nevertheless, the achievements of the college are considerable. More than half of its graduates go on to advanced study. Its stu-dents do well in garnering scholarships and fellowships (in con-trast to its early days of deprivation). It graduates a substantially higher proportion of its entering freshmen than the national aver-age. Its contribution to the ranks of young scholars is aston-ishingly high. In the entire country, Brooklyn College ranks sixteenth in having turned out B.A.'s between 1936 and 1956 who later attained the doctorate. In its statistical index (number of scholars per thousand graduates), Brooklyn ranks just below Amherst and Williams.

Among its alumni are Pulitzer Prize historian Oscar Handlin, comedian Sam Levenson, critic Irving Howe, stage star Alfred Drake, and a host of socially useful people. It includes also a lav-ishly contoured actress, who developed such a superb command of Romance languages at the college that she was able to palm herself off successfully in the film colony as an Italian bombshell right off the boat.

For thousands of its students, many of them first-rate, it is Brooklyn College or nothing. This is particularly true of the girls, a wasted resource we are beginning to realize, who have a low educational priority in most families. All in all, Brooklyn College is a stirring testament to America as an open society. Here is an authentic democracy of brains, and it works.

Dr. Harry D. Gideonse, president of the college, visited the Soviet Union a few summers ago and tells with relish of the Soviet official who fulminated against American colleges as instruments of class division. President Gideonse listened politely, then told him of the hundred-year-old system of free higher education in New York City. The Russian lapsed into stony silence.

Brooklyn College was established in the bleak economic weather of 1930. Beanie caps for freshmen sprouted amid the grimy office buildings of downtown Brooklyn where the college was housed in five implausibly scattered buildings. (The school song at the time had the wry title, "From the Portals of Joralemon to the Halls of Willoughby"—two buildings separated by a half-mile of commerce.)

If progressive education is the integration of theory and practice, then Brooklyn College had it in its pristine days. For the student was constantly jostled by the grubby facts of life. He made Chaplinesque changes of class—broadjumping the gutters, making hairbreadth escapes from onrushing cars, and bursting into the elevator at Court Street. Novelist Irwin Shaw recently wrote in the college magazine:

We had to ride in elevators crowded with shifty-eyed men talking about such low matters as mortgages and criminal nuisances, but the class in Elizabethan Drama Exclusive of Shakespeare was conducted in a room whose windows looked out on the harbor of New York, with the Statue of Liberty rearing up out of the green water and the big ships coming and going with their promise of a wider world than Brooklyn awaiting us. . . . If you were in love and the softness of a spring afternoon became unbearable, you could cut classes with your girl and walk to the end of Montague Street, where there was a small, paved park high over the docks and glittering bay.

And no alumnus, now thickening into middle-aged respectability, fails to mention the burlesque house across from one of the buildings whose fleshly enticements vied with General Chemistry II or Eighteenth-Century Thought.

Most colleges painstakingly build a tradition. Brooklyn College acquired one early in its history, repudiated it, and only a trace still exists. The tradition was that of student radicalism. During the thirties the campus reverberated with peace strikes, slogans ("Free Tom Mooney," "Fight Imperialist War"), and obscure factional disputes. The college newspaper was full of a gloomy and strident rhetoric. Playwright Norman Rosten recalls that some students, in an excess of working-class solidarity, picketed a local cafeteria whose workers were on strike. (It had been the hangout of all the little Lenins blueprinting American socialism over a slow cup of coffee.) A small disorder followed, and some of the students were arrested. "Sentence was later suspended," the alumnus recalls, "but the police blotter recorded what were perhaps the most unusual names in picketing history: Artur Schnabel, Becky Sharp, Titus Andronicus, and others." The political activity also had elements of adolescent horseplay. Peace strikes were the panty-raids of a solemn Depression generation.

An alumna of the thirties recalls how a frantic young man signaled her as he was being hauled into a "paddy wagon," after a political fracas. Pressing a nickel into her hand, he implored her to phone his mother. "Make up some excuse for me," he pleaded. "Don't tell her what happened!" The Boy Commissars, for all their truculence, were mama's sons in their warm little nests in Brownsville and Bensonhurst.

There was a fierce immigrant energy about the students then. "They were almost angry for knowledge," a faculty member recalls. And the legend of the intellectually belligerent, doggedly erudite student of the thirties persists to our own time.

In 1937 the college moved to its new quarters in Flatbush. It was the real thing—sweet-scented grass, red-brick buildings (however outsized), a small stadium, a library tower with gently pealing chimes. Student radicalism was at high tide, but it was the beginning of the end. President Gideonse, energetic and highly incisive, descended into the market place of ideas and carried on a tireless polemic against left-wing ideologues. (One of the college's livelier features during its combative days was the president's bulletin board on which he would anatomize the latest left-wing manifesto.) What is more he had in mind a long-range program of developing a college community which could shape value; otherwise, he argued, the emotional and spiritual vacuum would be exploited by totalitarians. A war-spawned prosperity supervened. More and more the college took on a middle-class coloring.

A story from 1946 epitomizes the change. A group of Brooklyn College girls were invited that year to one of those perennial student conferences at Vassar. The student movement still had some steam, and Brooklyn College, a working-class citadel, was viewed as the Holy City of student insurgency. The Vassar girls, uneasy about their wealth, dressed down conscientiously in sloppy jeans and waited for the arrival of the proletarian stalwarts. The delegation from Brooklyn College showed up—in Persian lamb and impeccable coiffures!

Small political explosions have occurred from time to time, but since World War II there has been no left-wing student movement of any notable dimensions. Brooklyn College, in a word, has become respectable. In contrast with its bitter, hungry days, its graduates move easily into medical schools, excellent graduate schools, and even into businesses formerly closed to them. Yet there is an admixture of pathos in all these gains. As the college has grown and improved, its image in the minds of students has declined. A distinguished scholar told me that when he went to Harvard for graduate work after Brooklyn back in the thirties, it was with "a sense of letdown." Harvard, after all, was a school for the idle rich, fatally indifferent to the march of history. And where but at Brooklyn or City College could one find a pure passion for learning uncontaminated by snobbery or careerism? (There was a quaint inverted snobbery in those days which equated poverty with virtue and honor.)

Academically, the standards of the college are far higher than they were twenty years ago during the Golden Age of the rebel-student. However, if class work is better, standards more rigorously professional, what goes on outside of class is of less intellectual account. During the thirties, formal class activity was less important than the ruthless thrashing out of ideas. The intellectual life had enormous leverage. Today's students are better academically, but the life of the mind excites less passion. The old energies survive chiefly in a fierce and unrelenting pursuit of grades, those shabby ikons which contaminate the curriculum.

The Brooklyn College student today has a sense of marginality. He is unhappy that he is denied that special badge of status—the out-of-town school. (He is realistic enough to know, however, that his training is as good as he can get anywhere.) Students talk carpingly about the impersonality of the school ("I didn't know it would be so IBM oriented . . . I was Number 14 in my Chem class"). The college lacks magic for them—it has always been part of the landscape of their lives—and the boys dream of undulant campus, and the Big Football Game, and an escape from sameness.

The college administration seems to share this wistfulness for the graces of the sleep-in school. It encourages students to do summer session work elsewhere, and permits them to amass more than 128 credits if they do. One summer recently, 631 students ran off to other groves of academe. The college also woos students from other campuses for its summer session, and proudly announces the presence on campus of academic sojourners from afar. A wasp-tongued student wrote me during the summer: "There are quite a few out-of-towners in attendance, and the school has bent backward to impress them with all sorts of concerts and a special bulletin *printed on rag paper*. Too good for the regular peasants, of course!"

One result of this sidelong glance at the out-of-town school is an extracurricular program which for sheer bulk and diversity may well surpass any in the country. Both Harvard and Sarah Lawrence are pallid by comparison. There are over three hundred student groups chartered by the college, and the House Plan Association is a small empire in itself. (Despite the name, the House Plan is simply a system of social clubs which have neither houses nor formal plans.) Among some students, there is an ambivalence about this roaring activity. They see it as compensatory for not being a campus school. "We're imitation Ivy League," a Dean's Honor List student said. Another boy observed, "There was no feast of ideas my first year. It was all social and House Plan."

The college offers this rationale: The students come from homogeneous backgrounds with limited opportunities for social expression. Moreover, the college is large, the atmosphere impersonal. There are many experiences outside of the classroom which these students need.

The academic program illustrates what David Riesman has termed the isomorphism of American colleges—the tendency to resemble each other. The pattern of General Education—a core of prescribed subjects and a functional major—has always prevailed at Brooklyn College, but it has undergone certain changes. A new curriculum was recently adopted whose principal feature is integrated courses in both social science and science.

The college is doing venturesome things with gifted students—an honors program and acceleration. President Gideonse has stated that "all real education is the fruit of self-study and that all effective teaching is concerned with helping the students to study by themselves."

Though the machinery for student-faculty consultation is limited, the good student has access to staff. "There is a kind of college within the college," a student remarked. "The faculty gets to know who the good students are, and there can be lots of contact."

Who are Brooklyn College students? What kind of homes do they come from? Sequestered in fiercely protective homes, comfortable only in their neighborhoods, college education for them is part of a large pattern of breakout. Their manners are often unpolished. "How do you endure them? They're thugs!" a professor fresh from a genteel women's college said heatedly. A few months later he was sitting around having coffee with his students in his free hours. He had responded, as other faculty members have, to their warmth and spontaneity and gusto.

They have a quenchless vitality; they are committed to life. A psychiatrist at a distinguished university was working on a study of student suicide rates. He invited Dean Herbert H. Stroup to participate in the study. "But we don't have suicide at Brooklyn College," Dean Stroup pointed out.

Less than half the students come from homes in which both parents are native-born. Most are Jewish (85 per cent), some are Catholic (11 per cent), and a smaller number are Protestant (4 per cent). There is a sprinkling of Negro students. The students

come from the world of small businessmen—increasingly beleaguered and worried—the retail storekeeper in an era of super-
markets, the salesman, and skilled worker. Family income is likely
to be unimpeachably middle-class, around $7,000 a year, but it is
a milieu which does not know the new security of the Organization Man. The families are warm, cohesive, and likely to be
packed into a small apartment. "There was always the TV going,"
a boy said, "and someone singing in the bathroom. I was going to
give up on getting my school work done, but somehow we
worked it out."

It is a tight little world despite its big city setting, carefully
shuttered from the outside. The students even have their own off-
campus beach. Bay 2 on Coney Island is their littoral "make-out"
center, swarming with adolescents who rarely go near the water
but are indefatigably social. Some Brooklyn College girls turn
down the opportunity for out-of-town colleges because of attach-
ment to family and friends. Few of these families have lived outside of New York. The parents hover protectively over their
children. (This is as characteristic of Italian parents as of Jewish
ones.) A father called one of the deans and wanted the "low-
down" on a boy who was courting his daughter. Mothers call the
administrative offices with frantic advice for their sons who left
their lunch at home. A woman whose boy was denied admission
threatened, "If I have a nervous breakdown, it'll be on your
head." It is a world at once cramped but intense, narrow but ex-
pressive. It has a disarming candor, a talent for forthright communication, and a passionate respect for learning.

Students are torn between devotion to these marvelously loyal
and self-sacrificing parents ("Everything for the children") and
resentment of their emotional parasitism. "As long as I'm home,
I'll never grow up," a nineteen-year-old girl said. A husky young
man observed sadly, "They don't like it if I do anything away from
home. It's so much trouble, I don't usually bother." Parents frequently drive to the college to pick up students who have stayed
for after-class activity.

There has been a changeover from Yiddish- or Italian-speaking
parents to *understanding* American ones. But this is merely a

substitution of a soft, reasonable tyranny for a hard one—the iron fist in the mental-hygiene glove.

In contrast with the thirties, there is little distance today between fathers and sons. The so-called conflict of culture has faded. Jewish college students no longer define themselves through rebellion against their parents. In fact, they often surpass their parents in the single-mindedness with which they pursue middle-class goals. (The *rapprochement* between the generations may well be symbolized by the changeover in the Catskill resort area. There used to be resorts for the "single crowd," reservations for the young in which they could act out their rebellion against the Puritanism of their parents. These resorts have been supplanted by plush family hotels where father, mother, and grown children can do their hedonistic cakewalk together.)

Before Christmas recess the college newspapers carry advertisements for package trips to Miami Beach. The size and glitter of engagement rings speak with as much authority for the young as for their elders. The most popular restaurant on campus is Wolfie's, blood kin to the Wolfie's of Miami Beach, where gastronomic excess is a high art. During winter intersession, a college-sponsored group goes to Grossinger's. There is a melancholy irony about this. For years there has been talk about countering the homogeneity of the students—"inbreeding" is the infelicitous term used. In the end, the massive ethnicism of the students triumphs—often in the wrong way.

However, the breakout from the cage of family and neighborhood takes place gradually. (For the out-of-town student it is implicit in that first flushed departure from home.) There are, to begin, the sorties into Manhattan, the rapt discovery of Greenwich Village (a quick phase) and the Museum of Modern Art (more enduring), the exotic adventures in strange restaurants. There is the strange vocabulary, the garish new ideas of higher education, which at once impress and discomfit the parents.

But the real breakout for those who do not marry while at college (those who do substitute the *gemütlich* despotism of the suburbs) is after college. Financial independence means a new burst of freedom—the summer run to Europe, the weekend ski trip, theater on Wednesday evening. Suddenly, the world lies open. As the final irrevocable step, there is the moving out of the parental home. The Brooklyn College provincial emerges from the chrysalis—a New York sophisticate.

Brooklyn is Herman Wouk territory. Any number of girls, radiant with self-discovery, announce, "I am Marjorie Morning-star." And indeed they are. There are hordes of nubile young women at Brooklyn College, ferociously determined to marry. There can be only one goal, nor should there be any unseemly tarrying en route. Go, girl, go, they say to each other. It is inter-esting that though the percentage of married students is no higher at Brooklyn than elsewhere—about 30 per cent of the women and 25 per cent of the men—the anxiety of the unmarried has puffed up the estimate. "Almost all the senior girls are married," stu-dents keep saying dogmatically.

While the Radcliffe girl chooses her major on its own merits, then makes modifications if she marries, the Brooklyn College girl often chooses hers—usually teaching—with a canny eye cocked at marriage. On the other hand, a Radcliffe girl said bluntly, "We're really just as eager to marry as the Brooklyn College girls. We just keep our mouths shut about it."

In any event, the House Plan Association, with its 150 chapters (men and women separate), is generally regarded as a teeming marriage mart. The Friday night House Plan party is de rigueur, and though students grind their teeth at its gaucheries ("It always starts out with boys on one side and girls on the other") they keep going—at least until they make it. "This is basic training for Grossinger's," a girl said grimly. Sometimes in a burst of ex-ogamy, House Plans will reach out to the exotic precincts of City College or New York University. The more enterprising women's houses will make contact with fraternities in medical or dental schools. Sometimes male House Plans are inveigled into parties with local high school girls, who, on the phone, successfully palm themselves off as a college sorority.

Kingsman, the college newspaper, sells space to jubilant houses, frats, and sororities with good news to impart. There are boxed announcements of watchings, pinnings, ringings, engagements, and marriages in a carefully graded hierarchy of felicity ("Witt

House happily announces the engagement of Fran Horowitz to Erwin Schwartz of Fife House"). There are sometimes modest little footnotes of upward mobility. If the lucky girl is marrying an out-of-town student, the boy's credentials will be duly cited in the box.

There is a healthy rivalry between the House Plan Association and the fraternity-sorority crowd. They vie with each other in good works for college and community. The House Plan, for example, sponsors an annual lecture by a distinguished outsider. However, charity abroad is spite at home. Some fraternity people characterize the House Plan as "the poor man's fraternity." They point out that House Plans have "rushes," and that there is almost as much straining for admission to choice houses as there is to a fraternity. House Planners counter by describing the Greeks as "camouflaged" houses. During rushing season, both groups buy space in *Kingsman* to attract shoppers. It may be an announcement of a smoker or a rush ("All dolls rush Dahl House"), or, in a calculated appeal to the power drive, the frat or sorority may cite the school big-shots in their ranks.

Most students agree, however, that at Brooklyn College a house *is* a home. "The House Plan is absolutely essential," a sophomore told me; "otherwise you're lost at school." In the meantime, Greek-letter societies seem to be expanding ("Go Fraternity," an ad in *Kingsman* exhorts), and some frats sweating out national affiliation are temporarily leading a schizoid existence (Delta Sigma Pi pending Sigma Delta Tau).

House Plans are often outgrowths of teen-age neighborhood social clubs. However, insularity breaks down in time. A house plan of girls from Brownsville, a working-class neighborhood, was reputed to have such bright and pretty girls that in time it attracted well-to-do Flatbush coeds. Most House Plans and Greek-letter societies tend to be self-segregating by color and religion, but there are some mixed groups.

There are almost a thousand more women than men attending Brooklyn College during the day—a tribute to the academic prowess of the girls in high school. (They do better at college, too.) The sexes are keenly responsive to each other, unlike Harvard's pattern of assiduous restraint. Brooklyn College boys have a frank appreciation of a pretty girl, and "making-out," the inelegant term for social success, is a status-building pursuit. However, the sexes complain about each other. The girls talk petulantly about the boys' lack of gallantry. (A boy retorted, "I tried to hold a door open for a girl, but she was too fast for me.") The boys, just beginning to taste the heady joys of young manhood, resent the girls' rage to marry ("They race to the hunt"). The boxes announcing the intramural engagements and marriages would suggest that the hostilities are successfully surmounted.

The Brooklyn College girl is yoked to middle-class respectability, and the drama of her chastity is a solemn matter. Because she lives at home and accepts her family's values, she is probably less venturesome about sex than many college students elsewhere. It is against this background that one can appreciate an episode that occurred a few years ago. With its usual éclat, the theater group was doing a performance of García Lorca's *The House of Bernarda Alba*. It was Saturday night, which attracts the student-dating crowd, a notoriously volatile audience. The climactic moment of the play, heart-rending in its intensity, is when the black-clad mother of an errant maiden shrieks, "Tell them in the city my daughter is a virgin!" There was a stunned silence for a moment, and then the audience of dating couples broke down helpless with laughter.

Brooklyn College is distinctive for not having an *official* drinking place. There are bars nearby, but they are not frequented by students. A drink is something a student nurses along on a Saturday-night date at a dine-and-dance place. "I drink to be sociable" is the usual pronouncement. Dancing, however, is another matter. And the Byzantine flourishes one sees in cha-cha-cha or mambo at a Brooklyn College dance would give an Arthur Murray instructor a pained sense of inadequacy.

The topography of the cafeteria is as complex and colorful as that of any student union in the country. Through a mysterious process of acculturation, students learn where to sit. The cafeteria is terra incognita to faculty, and only through the assistance of a student cicerone was I able to get an inside view. One side of the huge, tumultuous room is for frats and sororities with "some strays in the back." There is a theater table appropriately located stage front (near the serving line where everyone passes). Then there are the special-interest groups—Newman Club, athletics, and even a non-belongers' table. House Plans are everywhere.

The student lounges reflect that curious bifurcation in the psyche of the American student as he strains for well-roundedness. There used to be two: the Popular Lounge, and the Classical Lounge. The former is the hangout of the "lounge majors," as well as the casual student with half an hour to kill. There is usually an insistent musical beat as the "hip-collegiates," who occupy a kind of halfway house to hipsterism, do their frozen-faced mambos. The Classical Lounge, now pre-empted by the bookstore, provided serious music, chess sets, and an air of inviolate gravity. *Kingsman* recently suggested that the Popular Lounge turn its back on fun for a few hours a week to play the music of the masters. It asked, "Doesn't a mixture of the classics and pop music go hand-in-hand with the principles of a broad liberal arts education?"

There seems to be far more individuality at Brooklyn College than I observed elsewhere. In fact, individuality has to be tough and rugged just to escape being crushed by the sheer numbers at Brooklyn College. The boys range from impeccable Ivy League types, replete with bristling crew-cuts, chinos, and buckskin shoes, to a shaggy-headed youth discussing absurdity in Camus with a cigarette tucked behind his ear truck-driver style. The girls dress with great variety—smartly garbed ones looking as if they have a modeling engagement after class (some do), the great mass of neatly and inconspicuously dressed ones, and those who proclaim their protest by wearing sneakers or desert boots.

Because the college community is large and amorphous, there is an absence of faddishness both in life-style and in ideas. In the measure that the college fails as a community—and this is inevitable in a subway school—it does nothing to discourage the rich diversity of the students. There are the House Planners and the grinds; the folk singers on the library steps on Friday afternoon, and the ultra-Orthodox Jewish boys wearing skullcaps. And one-third of the school's population has no commerce with extracurricular activity and are touched only by the ideas they encounter in class.

Brooklyn College students often start out with only a limited sense of their own possibilities. They have little to define themselves against, no college tradition (such as Harvard's), little knowledge of any milieu but their own. But when they achieve liberation from the tight confines of their world, they are the richer for having been immured. They have a vivid sense of what they have left behind and what they have gained. There are advantages in bestriding many worlds. It yields a rich harvest in perception, irony, and humor.

The faculty is well paid, carefully selected, and able. Teaching schedules are heavier than in other first-rate schools, and this has some effect on scholarly production. Students complain that they do not have sufficient personal contact with their teachers. ("They race us to the door," one student said.) This, however, is only partly true. A student who seeks such contact can find it, especially in his major. But, in truth, the crowds and the bustle, the staff rooms housing five and six instructors, do not encourage a leisurely exchange between faculty and students. Moreover, many of the students work after school and have little time to loaf and invite their souls.

Only the naive believe that life on a college campus is tranquil. Universities are large bureaucracies today with built-in tensions. Brooklyn College is probably no better and no worse than most. Among the administrators, there is a brave show of unanimity. The faculty, however, is merrily schismatic. In a delicious irony, the Philosophy Department has been particularly discordant. A faculty wag, who has watched their Donnybrooks from a safe distance, described them as "lovers of wisdom and haters of each other." In any event, the only way a factional dispute could be resolved was to appoint as chairman a talented member of the English Department with a sideline in philosophy.

To the ordinary hazards of academic life must be added the Kafkaesque terrors of coping with such faceless entities as city budgets, state legislation, and the Board of Higher Education, all of which influence the city colleges.

Counseling is one of the major devices used to counter the large size and impersonality of the college. Some years ago, a senior asked Dean William R. Gaede for a recommendation to graduate school. The dean asked who knew him. "No one," the student answered. That was the beginning of counseling.

It is an ambitious program of guidance embracing general (or curriculum) counseling, personal counseling, and guidance in one's major field. To avoid professional parochialism, faculty members are enlisted into the general counseling program on a part-time basis. A recent survey revealed that 52 per cent of the students said that they benefited from the program, 31 per cent were unfriendly, and 16 per cent were undecided. Students in private discussion had varied and vigorous reactions. Much seemed to hinge on the individual counselor. A bright young woman was ablaze with admiration for her counselor's skill and devotion. Another student said peremptorily, "I don't like him. I don't want him, but I can't get rid of him." A student with a personal problem waited one year to be seen. ("That's one form of therapy," an administrator said wryly.) Another, in the hands of an assiduous general counselor, was referred for personal counseling in a matter of days.

The purpose of personal counseling, according to its supervisor, is "to see to it that inefficiencies do not flow from emotional problems." It is not the idea of salvaging the psychotic but helping the normal individual to fulfill his potential. Problems may range from minor disturbances—inability to concentrate or family conflict—to the tragi-comic psychic dislocation of the student who wrote: "Request return to Brooklyn College to take Abnormal Psychology provided I can wear shoes and stockings and suit to school, take a shower regularly, and take a strict physical exam from the Hygiene Department."

Because it is a new program, there has been some resistance to counseling on the part of the staff. To some faculty members, Personnel Service is the new monolith on campus. The smiling emissaries from Teachers College are viewed with suspicion. "Too often," President Gideonse explained, "instructors are interested only in the potential little mathematician or economist." It may be that the Department of Personnel Service has too much missionary zeal and is overly enchanted by its grand designs. Certainly, its official language has a stubborn gracelessness with phrases like "consultative relationships," "counseling locales," and "goal maintenance" running riot. Some people point out that this department with its twenty-eight members looms too large in a college in which the Philosophy Department numbers only twelve and Political Science twenty-three.

Recurrently, there are conflicts between the students and the administration. A school official said grimly, "I run around with a hose like a fireman putting out a blaze." The edginess of the students may be a carrying forward into a nonpolitical era of the old aggressions of the thirties. The fight for Bermuda shorts (currently banned for on-campus wear) may well be the de-based student movement of the sixties. Or, as one faculty member suggested, ambivalences about family are displaced on to the college administration. (A recent study revealed, interestingly enough, that young Brooklyn College graduates now teaching identify more with their pupils than with the principals and assistant principals of their schools.)

Certainly the old political fervors are quiescent. Even as re-spectable an enterprise as "Sane Nuclear Policy" could round up only 175 signatures for a petition. Many were afraid to sign ("Look, I plan to teach; I'll give you money, but don't ask me to sign"), although the college administration did nothing to discourage the campaign. There are about sixty students in all the political groups with about fifteen in a socialist club, but as a Young Democrat sardonically observed, "All they do is sit around and watch their beards grow."

Periodically there is a flare-up over the school newspaper. Since *Kingsman* is a "monopoly newspaper" supported by student fees, the prevailing policy is that of "multiple simultaneous edi-torials" to insure presentation of opposing points of view. "Brook-lyn College does not charter two or more newspapers, as is the case in Queens or City College," President Gideonse has argued. "Thomas Jefferson's idea about freedom did not refer to a monop-olistic press that was supported by required fees. They referred to a competitive press which was self-supporting." A few years ago, *Kingsman*'s editors resigned over the workings of this policy. Their parting editorial shot was called, dramatically, "A Cup of Hemlock." ("I learned that the race for an assistant professorship in Brooklyn College is as bad as the race for assistant vice-president on Madison Avenue. . . . I learned that freedom of the press is taught in classrooms only to be untaught in the President's office.")

There is an inchoate student feeling about being fussed over too much. One wonders if they do not sense some subtle rejection in the administration's nervous vigilance about their behavior, dress, etc. Some expressed resentment at the presence of hostesses who supervise the lunchroom. Others vented animus against the Student Activities Office, which, according to one student, has a beatific vision of all Brooklyn College girls in short hair looking like Vassar girls. Tea has become the symbol of a quiet tug-of-war. The joke among the rebel fringe who resist the genteel *Gleichschaltung* is that all they drink at "teas" is coffee. And one student told with relish of setting up a tea for her organization and asking for two urns of coffee. Her adviser was aghast. "Won't you take even a small pot of tea?" she implored.

These issues in a college in swift transition are complex. The concern about student's dress, for example, grew out of the Placement Office's observation that the students are deficient in this area, and that it costs them dear when applying for jobs. Moreover, Brooklyn College is a tax-supported institution, and in effect, every taxpayer is a trustee, some of them highly obstreperous ones. In back of the recent dress-up campaign, too, were letters written by subway passengers about the inappropriate dress of a handful of students. (A "dress-right" campaign was organized to "set patterns of expectancy." A student leader, eagerly opting for the Organization world, said, "We've got to re-orient the orienters.")

My own experience as faculty advisor of a student magazine is instructive. A relatively mild story about a love affair—far milder than a story in Harvard's *Advocate* which someone there gave me to read—elicited a semiliterate and hysterical letter from a maiden lady in the community. In a rapture of illogic, she suggested that Brooklyn College students "must be Communist since they are obscene." It was suggested to me by a college official that I ought to encourage "more cheerful stories." That such a letter should even be taken seriously points up the problem of a tax-supported institution. "Let's do our job," a colleague of mine said testily, "and let the chips fall where they may."

Forty-two per cent of the college's students are preparing to teach in elementary or secondary schools. A sometimes angry debate rages on campus about the effect of this teacher-training program. Some people argue that the intellectual tone of the college has been impaired by the heavy concentration of education majors. The standard criticism is that "Ed" courses are ineffective and sentimental, jargon-ridden and repetitive. ("I'm tired of the whole child, the half-child, and the quarter-child," a prospective teacher said.) There is an ideological bent in the Education Department which some faculty members find disconcerting. There seems to be the implication that there is a crisp right or wrong in every situation. The pedagogy crowd is alleged to have contempt for a skeptical or tragic view of human experience. Education is a peculiarly American field of study, and it has a blatantly happy-ending, upbeat point of view.

A girl chemistry major dismissed Brooklyn College scornfully as "Flatbush State Teachers College." "Mothers," she argued, "push their daughters into college because, after all, 'a college boy wants a college girl.' So what do they major in? Education! Of course, they may hate kids. So what?"

Defenders of the Education Department have some telling arguments, although they do acknowledge excesses ("There are progressives and manic-progressives"). For one thing, Brooklyn College represents a pattern of teacher education within a liberal arts framework. That means that teachers are likely to be a good deal better educated here than they would be in a teacher-training college. If Ed majors seem undeveloped intellectually this cannot be ascribed to the Education Department alone, since they carry only from 20 to 40 credits out of 128 in education.

Part of the prejudice against the department is traceable to its rapid growth at the expense of other departments. Then, too, the department has no clear-cut intellectual credentials. It is an omnibus department consisting of people with training in sociology, psychology, and philosophy, as well as in education.

Some hard thinking is taking place about the future. Proposals vary from creating a separate school of education (which would probably have a down-grading effect on Ed majors) to giving prospective teachers a straight liberal arts program with education courses segregated in a fifth year of study. Another proposal comes close to the Sarah Lawrence pattern—exemption from Ed courses to be attained by a process of self-study. It has also been suggested that Ed majors be required to take a good solid minor of at least twelve credits in a demanding subject matter area. (The tendency at present is for Ed majors to nibble at snap courses when taking free electives.)

The evening session is steeped in an atmosphere reminiscent of harder times. Here students and faculty share a common martyrdom of late hours, gulped meals, and strenuous intellectual exercise at war with fatigue. Something of the tradition of pure intellectual passion survives here. Students in the evening—generally older than their daytime colleagues of the bright sweaters and scuffed shoes—are regarded as more serious. ("There are *students* in the evening," a young man summed up. "In the day they are *pupils*.") Courses are sometimes less demanding as a result of teacher's compassion, but the students bring maturity and experience often surpassing the teacher's. The charm of the evening classes is in the rich variety of types: salesmen and police officers, stenographers and housewives exultantly on leave from baby and kitchen. There was one garment center model who used to come sweeping into class in a glory of color and perfume. In five years of attendance she was transformed into a somber-eyed intellectual drone in flats.

There is also the pathos of the many nonmatriculated students —nine out of ten of these ultimately drop out—who come to the college with the stubborn democratic faith that anybody, no matter how gross his ineptitude, can be a college student.

Brooklyn College is a young institution caught up in a fast-paced drama of social change. It may be that the college in response to a genuine need has gone too far in "socializing" its students at the cost of images of daring and sacrifice. Too much, perhaps, is predicated on "getting into graduate school" or being acceptable to employers. At this time, there is little in the college to generate a creative and responsible criticism of society.

A recent episode illustrates the curious student temper of our time. Jack Kerouac, the high priest of the Beat Generation, came to talk at Brooklyn College. He arrived at 9:30 P.M. to confront a swarm of students—most of them from the day session—who had waited hours for him. Some were avid apprentices of the Beat Generation, blue-jeaned boys and black-stockinged girls. Hundreds came out of curiosity but not curiosity alone. They came out of some deep yearning for the Word. To my amazement, when the program began notebooks were solemnly opened, pens were poised.

Kerouac was frivolous. "What's your outlook on life?" a student asked. "It's an illusion—not real, man: you ought to know that," the writer answered. A girl asked, "Why do you believe in Buddhism?" "Why are you so pretty?" he responded. The students were indignant. They stayed and listened but they felt cheated. Underneath what someone has described as "the gloriously contented air" of the contemporary college student, there is an unsatisfied need to know and to believe.

In the spring of 1960 there was a resurgence of a spirit that everyone thought was softly extinct. Some students, at least, threw off the encircling apathy. The campus resounded with old alarums and excursions. The House Plan Association, hardly notable for its political passions, came out in support of the Southern lunchroom sit-in movement. A student editor was suspended from his post for an editorial which talked grimly of the "lies of deans." A Civil Defense drill provoked deliberate and organized civil disobedience. Forty-three students were suspended for four days, but it was largely a token punishment since these absences were not to be counted if the students were over-cut. Nevertheless, students protested that the administration was "legally right but morally wrong." In the midst of this tumult the editor of *Kingsman* resigned because of alleged censorship. (A student photographer had been forbidden to take a photo of those boycotting the Civil Defense drill.) Free press rallies—with permission granted by the administration—took place on campus.

However, there were illuminating contrasts with earlier episodes of student insurgency. There was a certain self-consciousness about these gentle revolts. "The current free press rallies," the student newspaper declared, "are the one fresh breath of air in a stale atmosphere." Students hovered over the sacred flame of militancy as if it might go out any moment. And one campus newspaper sighed uneasily that the summer quietus would probably snuff out these first faint stirrings of protest.

And even the guerrilla fighters are a new breed. Other-directed rebels, they profess to understand the position of the administrators. ("After all," one student told me, "they have to impose *some* punishment.") And canny strategists, the punishment secretly pleases them, for otherwise what would the protest movement feed on? The radicals of another era—all fierce defiance, angry slogan, and howling anathema—would be mystified by all this.

In the meantime, the college goes about its business: providing a first-rate education for first-rate students. Campus *Lebensraum* is slowly being swallowed up by concrete as new buildings rise. But the academic zeal, which makes for such a vivid experience for both teacher and student, is in no danger of being entombed.

PARSONS COLLEGE: Little School with Big Ideas

American colleges are caught in a painful two-way squeeze. On the one hand, there is increasing pressure from hordes of young people—and their frantic parents—for admission to college. And the tidal wave has yet to hit. On the other hand, colleges are notoriously insolvent, and the more students they take in, the bigger their deficits. Everybody shakes his head sadly and says that the situation will get worse before it gets better.

But does it have to? Or are answers already visible on the horizon? Some colleges have begun to spin away from their lethargy. And one of the most energetic and forthright in tackling its problems is Parsons College, a small school in a sleepy Iowa town.

It faced dour circumstances in 1955. Its enrollment had shriveled, and it was heavily in debt. Sluggish, neglected, demoralized, it was another academic backwater. In five years, this little Presbyterian college underwent a striking face lifting and quickening of spirit. It now has 1,400 students (with lots of applicants clamoring at the gates), it is bursting with financial health, and it is doing new and interesting things educationally. "The fastest growing college in the country" is the way it describes itself.

Parsons is not one of America's great colleges. It doesn't pretend to be. It doesn't even *want* to be—if that means being a school for the elite top 10 per cent. But it provides a bracing object lesson in what a small school can do through a blend of imagination, daring, and sturdy common sense. And it's worth pointing out that about half of this country's thousand colleges are small (under five hundred students), obscure, and financially pressed. They would be well advised to take a careful look at what Parsons has wrought.

Parsons deserves a good, hard look for another reason. We have gone overboard about *quality* in higher education. High school seniors beat their fists bloody trying to get into top-drawer schools. And the best colleges send out talent scouts to round up scholastic prodigies. In the process, the average youngster tends to get lost and discouraged. Parsons is distinctive in that it has a stubborn affection for the non-genius, for the pleasant, wholesome average student—even for the marginal one. And it is determined to give him a crack at a first-rate education with first-rate teachers. With an admirable sense of fair play, it says: "Let's give them a *chance* at higher education. Let's even give them *another* chance if they have failed elsewhere."

Located in Fairfield, in southeastern Iowa, Parsons College comprises fifty-five green and pleasant acres, with old, musty buildings, and a gentle, somnolent flavor. ("The Midwest," a faculty member said tartly, "is the tranquilizer of the nation.") Fairfield is a farm and manufacturing center built around the usual courthouse square. Its old-fashioned character can be gleaned from the hotel rooms, which have ropes coiled in their closets. Their purpose: in case of fire, the hotel patron ties the rope to his bed and, in time-honored fashion, lowers himself out the window to safety.

The college is set at the northern end of town. Next to the football field is a meadow in which a herd of cattle munch unmindful of the educational cataclysm swirling about them. A coed recently went to practice on the organ in the chapel only to discover that an enormous white horse had preceded her there. She did not tarry to find out whether he had come to pray, listen to the organ, or find grass.

It's a friendly school. A boy with a new jazz record will rush to the home of a professor known to be a jazz buff. On Campus Day, faculty and students alike drop their books, pick up rakes and brooms, and spruce up the college grounds. A professor who attended a fashionable college remarked: "At _____ College, I saw faculty and students play the little game of who-destroys-whom. I have never seen it here." When a former Miss America, the girl friend of the football coach, came to visit, the campus was in a paroxysm of excitement. (And there was widespread lamentation when she broke the engagement, and glamor vanished from the campus.)

There is the usual round of college fun: football, Homecoming, dances, a marching and pep band, fraternities and sororities. In a word, Parsons is superficially like hundreds of other small colleges in the hinterland—with this big difference: it has solved its financial problems. It has a powerful sense of forward motion. "The difference between Parsons and other small colleges in Iowa," a student observed, "is that the future here is bright and foreseeable."

Let's start at the beginning. In 1955 the college faced its darkest hour. It was heavily in debt, it was down to 212 students (mostly local), and its average faculty salary was a paltry $3,700 a year. In short, it was gasping its last.

The picture today is fantastically different. Parsons has a student body of 1,450 (with a huge freshman class of 750), drawn from 25 states and 10 foreign countries. Over 52 per cent of the faculty have earned doctorates, which places it in the upper 5 per cent of all colleges. (It also represents a 400 per cent increase over five years ago.) Its salary scale, particularly for a small Midwestern school, is princely with a median of $7,200, putting Parsons in the same salary class as the haughty schools in the East and in the upper 2 per cent of Midwestern institutions. The debt load has been banished, and the physical plant of the campus has doubled in value. Moreover, Parsons is one of the few colleges which defray all operating expenses from tuition. The drop-out rate, which used to be a demoralizing 61 per cent, is down to a respectable 15 per cent. And as a symbol of this proud new era in its history, the college is applying this year for a Phi Beta Kappa chapter.

Of course, it has its limitations. "Parsons is no Iowa Yale," a spokesman said. Its experience offers no panacea for *all* the vexatious problems which make the job of college president so precarious. (*Their* drop-out rate is frightful.) But there is no doubt that in its spunky facing up to its problems, Parsons has something to teach American colleges.

How did this miracle on the prairie take place? Probably the biggest single factor is Parsons president Dr. Millard G. Roberts, a forty-two-year-old Presbyterian minister, ex-football player, Navy chaplain, teacher—a man as adroit with a financial statement as with a sermon. Pudgy, flamboyant, tireless, Roberts has the glad-handing manner of a Chamber of Commerce president, the force of a bulldozer, and the guile, when the college requires it, of a snake-oil salesman. "He'll step out of a Chamber of Commerce meeting where he's giving a pep talk," a professor said, "and go to a humanities lecture and talk brilliantly about St. Augustine." And he has ideas—practical, hard-headed ideas—about what ails colleges and how these ailments can be cured.

He directs his educational revolution from a redecorated office in Parsons Hall. All around him are portraits of former presidents —bearded worthies, almost all of whom, significantly, had short tenures. They seem to look on with a mixture of dismay and envy.

Taking his cues from the Ruml Report on the reorganization of higher education, Roberts went through Parsons like a whirlwind. He killed sacred cows, he smashed worn-out educational ikons, he brought in new good people, and drove out old, incompetent ones. He was tough, rough, and ruthless, but he saved Parsons College from a genteel demise.

This is what he did. He applied the principles of good corporate management to higher education—an outrageous notion to old-line educators. Most colleges boast about its low student-teacher ratio. Parsons brags about its high one. The ratio climbed from 7 to 1 in 1955 to the current 20 to 1. That means that tuition now covers the expense of instruction. (And tuition has gone up to $600 a year. With room and board, an academic year at Parsons comes to $1,500—a modest enough figure these days.)

It is Roberts' conviction that faculty, not buildings, makes a college. And so he has recruited good people—usually in their thirties—with Ph.D.'s or close to it. And this has paid off. Parsons students talk about the percentage of earned doctorates in the faculty with the knowing air of college deans.

"Why should you pay a professor full salary for teaching three kids in one class and four in another?" asked industrialist Richard Hoerner, chairman of the Board of Trustees. Parsons professors now teach full classes and full programs. This is insured by cutting the number of courses from 755 to 169. The average teaching load this year is twelve hours a week (plus tutoring), an improvement over last year's punishing nineteen hours weekly.

Professors at Parsons are rewarded by being permitted to live in a pleasant little welfare state. They work hard, but the college is generous with loan money for homes, it subsidizes graduate study through sabbaticals with full pay, and every faculty member is automatically a member of the local country club. In addition, the college looks with favor on teaching couples on the sound premise that two academic incomes are better than one.

The college steered around the necessity of erecting new buildings by using the plant almost on an around-the-clock basis, with classes in the morning, afternoon, on Saturdays—even during lunch hour.

Roberts is, avowedly, an Organization Man, and he has not hesitated to expand the administrative apparatus of the college. Early in his tenure, the school was actually spending more on administrative personnel than for faculty—an intolerable heresy to most educators. Administrative expense jumped from $83,000 to $150,000 in a three-year period, as against only $229,000 for instruction. Now that the enrollment and faculty are so much larger, the proportion of the budget allocated to administration is more reasonable.

There are five admissions counselors, regarded, frankly, as "procurement men." They scour the country and stimulate interest in Parsons among high school students and guidance counselors. "We've got to keep our salesmen on the road," Roberts said bluntly. He is himself a one-man task force in the selling department. On the road three or four days a week, he travels 100,000 miles a year, and gives over 250 speeches—including commencement addresses—with a view towards building up the image of the college. And the way he works is a small triumph of strategy. He turns up at a high school, gives a stirring talk about education, and provokes interest in this lively little college in the back country. Next, promotional material about Parsons starts to infiltrate. When a psychological beachhead is secured, an admissions counselor moves in.

Parsons is, unashamedly, a football school—not out of any passion for the bruising sport but because of its promotional value. "Circling us are big cities like Chicago, Omaha, Peoria, and Minneapolis," Roberts explained. "We want more students from these cities. You get one thousand inches of space from football for one inch from a scholarly article by a professor."

Another essential in the Parsons scheme of things is a strong board of trustees. In the Roberts administration, thirteen trustees, dismayed by the new winds blowing, resigned; eighteen new ones were added. The board consists of 80 per cent businessmen, 10 per cent educators, and 10 per cent clergymen. They are largely men of substance, and as Roberts proudly said, "They have money to put where their mouth is." (Gift money goes for buildings, since tuition takes care of operating costs.) "Trustees see their function," the president pointed out, "as checking up on me. They own the place. But once policy is set, they never stick their noses in."

Unlike previous boards, this group meets regularly, sometimes in Fairfield but often in Chicago or Des Moines—"places where they can get their planes in," Roberts added significantly.

One of the most exciting—and controversial—features of Parsons is the program for marginal students. Unlike other schools which compete fiercely only for topnotch students, Parsons woos the weak and discouraged. One-third of all new students are either from the lower half of their class or flunkees from other colleges.

Roberts makes a spirited case for the admission of marginal students. Marks and test scores are inaccurate measures of a student's potential, he argues, and they rarely reflect the unique gifts of youngsters who are imaginative and creative. Then there are the "late bloomers" and the hapless victims of sloppy elementary and high school education.

"There are 204 high schools in Iowa," Roberts explained, "with four teachers or less. There are often three graduates in these schools—a valedictorian, a salutatorian, and a dumbbell. The dumbbell may wind up as a marginal student in Parsons."

There is also a religious argument that he invokes in favor of the marginal program. "God created all men and loves all of them as part of His plan," he says. "And our action is one way through which God's will is made real today." All he is doing, Roberts asserts, is delaying the final selection of college students for a few years. His clinching argument is that a "secret poll" of his own trustees—solid men glittering with success—revealed the astonishing fact that many of them were barely C students in college.

Horace Sutton, librarian at Parsons, is another partisan of the marginal plan and offers himself in evidence. He had flunked out at the University of California, then went on to earn a Phi Beta Kappa key at Kenyon College, an equally demanding institution. "I'm very proud of this key," he said fingering the gold symbol of his redemption hanging from his key chain.

Roberts summed up the college's position: "As long as a student has ten dollars in his pocket, the desire to get through, and a willingness to work, I believe Parsons should find a place for him."

But the school paces these students through some strenuous academic push-ups. Marginal students must devote one preliminary semester to workshops, tutoring, and orientation. The workshops repair the educational damage of earlier years—sometimes by reaching back to fifth grade spelling lists or eighth grade arithmetic. Orientation teaches students how to study, outline material, prepare for exams, and budget their time—basic equipment in the student's toolkit.

And the program seems to work. That is the most heartening part of it. Of eighty-six transfer students in 1959–1960, none of whom had attained a C average previously, four attained a straight A standing, thirty-three had averages above B, and only eight were below C. A husky youth transferred from a small college in California, where he received all D's and F's except for an A in baseball. (This immediately conjures up the image of the dumb athlete.) "I woke up to the fact that you've got to have an education to get anywhere," he said. "That degree really opens the door. My waking up was brought about by people at Parsons. In California if you got low grades, then you got low grades. Here they talk to you about it."

To prevent the down-drag of marginal students, the college pulls from the other end by bringing in bright students on scholarship. Nor does the presence of marginal students truly represent a decline in standards at Parsons. "In the old days," a veteran professor said bluntly, "we couldn't afford to let failing students leave. We held on to them. Today we don't have to." Marginal students who don't make the grade in two semesters are asked not to return.

The program has its critics. "It's all right," a student said, "but I wish they wouldn't play it up so much." Some students began to call Parsons "the dummy school" after an article in a Des Moines newspaper described it as a last-hope alley for flunkees. "It's a vicious thing for some and wholesome for others," a new faculty member summed up. "Some kids are simply not college material and are wasting their money. For others it works."

There is criticism of the workshops often as overcrowded as the classrooms whose casualties they are designed to save. But that, Roberts has argued, is merely one of the "bugs" that a college, in swift transition, has to straighten out.

At the other end of the academic spectrum, Parsons has introduced an ambitious great-books program similar to that of the University of Chicago. (Dr. Roberts received his Ph.D. there in history, and his wife, also a Ph.D., taught the great books at Chicago.) Every student takes a one-credit humanities course each semester. Thirty-two great books are read in full or in part during the four-year sequence. The purpose is to "create a vital intellectual unity within the College." Towards that end, *all* professors, in suitably mated teams, teach in the program. (Imagine the football coach lecturing on Aristotle!) It has its problems, to be sure. Some professors, in alien territory, are fearful of exposing their ignorance. Others feel that the courses encourage a cheap dilettantism. And many students have carried on a guerrilla warfare against the program—mostly in protest against a lot of reading for one meager credit. (They even burned

Homer in effigy one evening.) There is scornful talk of the easy tests and how simple it is to get by merely by reading synopses.

But the program has its ardent champions, too. A chemistry professor said, "In graduate school, I didn't read outside my field. But last year I worked harder on Thucydides than on chemistry." The baseball coach, as a result of his experience in the program, is taking broad, cultural Ph.D. courses instead of the usual narrow physical education stuff. Perhaps the most realistic view was offered by an English professor to his students: "The humanities program won't make you a better engineer or doctor. But between the second and third cocktail, when someone mentions Plato, you'll at least know what he's talking about."

The latest Parsons innovation is the trimester plan adopted June 1960. Other colleges have mulled over the idea endlessly, but Parsons went ahead with it. The plan involves three semesters of seventeen weeks each, including a full summer semester. (The trick during the summer, according to Roberts, is to air-condition the library only and send the students running pell-mell there.) According to the plan, Parsons will be able to accommodate two thousand students, although at any given time there won't be more than fourteen hundred men and women on campus.

Its virtue is its remarkable flexibility. Eager beavers, in a hurry to do graduate work or get married, can sprint through their work in two and two-thirds years, while dawdlers can take the usual four years with summers off. For the marginal student, there is the extra semester each year in which to catch up and make up. And for the others, there are exciting new possibilities: a semester abroad, a term of work in the fall at a time when college students are not flooding the labor market, and one traditional take-it-easy summer.

This is how a four-year program would work: Freshmen will study for three consecutive semesters followed by a fall semester on a job. (The job is designed to diverge radically from the student's course of study and from his background. Thus, an Iowa farm girl majoring in education might go to work in a metropolitan area in the office of a large corporation.) The student will return for the spring term and have his only summer vacation. In his junior year, he can go abroad for seventeen weeks, followed by three semesters of academic work culminating in graduation in June.

How has the Parsons faculty reacted to this permanent revolution raging around their bewildered heads? One thing making for professorial acquiescence is simply cold cash. When Roberts arrived and confronted an $800,000 deficit, his first act was to raise salaries 30 per cent—a bold gesture and an effective one.

"I'm getting more money than I ever thought I would see at Parsons," a professor said. "When I came here in 1935, I had to keep a cow in the backyard in order to live. And I milked her every evening between sets of papers. With money you can do things, go places."

"You teach in a room that has been discolored for ten years," another teacher remarked, "and Roberts comes along and has it painted."

"Things are happening so fast around here," an English professor observed, "the faculty doesn't have time to brood. Where I used to teach, we spent lots of time amending amendments. Here we're too busy for such nonsense."

The hectic pace is illustrated by this exchange. "What's new?" a professor asked his friend. "I don't know," his colleague answered. "I've been away for two hours."

Faculty democracy is a victim of the new era. Some professors miss it, although as one man said, "I'm sure we did all sorts of dumb things in the name of faculty self-determination." Today the college is run by the president and the trustees, as the Ruml Plan suggests. Nobody is fired outright—Roberts respects tenure —but as a professor pointed out, "When you don't get raises, and don't get praises, you ultimately resign."

"Roberts wants them to teach, teach, teach," an observer remarked. "In return, he gives them security and good money. But the pattern is such that it restricts the visibility of the faculty since they don't have time to research or publish." (In 1958–1959 there were only five scholarly articles published by the entire faculty.) Roberts counters with the argument that in the trimester program, faculty will have full semesters to devote to graduate study or do research. But the nub of the matter is that Parsons is essentially a teaching college, not a growth of knowl-

edge center. It can provide few answers for the problems be-
setting large universities, where a low student-teacher ratio is a
necessary condition for research productivity.

There are those who grumble that the college is a one-man
show. "Roberts is overbearing and ruthless in an unbelievable
way," a professor said, "but because he's a clergyman you're taken
by surprise." He allegedly rides roughshod over faculty opposition and has publicly humiliated his enemies. He is charged with
having a swollen ego, with playing fast and loose with statistics,
and with being more promoter than educator—"more blow than
show" is the way one critic put it. His inauguration as president,
for which an imposing $10,000 was spent, was dubbed "The
Ascension." Roberts smilingly admits the expense and insists it
was worth the publicity it yielded. But the real question is
whether the miracle at Parsons could have occurred without
Roberts' drive and rough-hewn tactics.

Then there are those who brood about whether the principles
of good corporate management should be applied to higher education. "Professors are not bright young executives going up the
gray flannel ladder," a Parsons teacher said. "You're likely to be
judged here for administrative efficiency and not for the traditional things that really count. It can create a certain malaise."

Parsons students, along with pride in their school's upward
surge, feel a certain uneasiness. They resent their president's aggressive energy as much as they admire it. "We discussed the
school colors," a student leader recalled, "but we discovered that
Dr. Bob had already ordered the new flag." They are disturbed
by having an absentee president. "He's in about fourteen states
every month," a boy said. "He ought to reserve three or four days
for us." And for a school which makes such a fetish of public
relations, communication between administration and students is
curiously inadequate. "We had to read *The Des Moines Register*
to find out about the marginal student policy," a girl remarked.
Finally, the slambang growth of the college has created disquietude. "We didn't know why some of us had to live in
kitchens and hallways, why there were five guys to a desk, and
why the roof leaked," an angry young man complained.

Parsons has shot up like a giant. With forced growth, educational quality—a delicate, tender thing—can be bruised or crushed. It can be argued that this has happened at Parsons. On the other hand, a live, lusty college has a better chance of achieving the loftiest goals of education than one dying at the roots, as Parsons undoubtedly was only five years ago. Dr. Roberts and his trustees have demonstrated how a college can survive—and prosper. Institutions of higher learning the length and breadth of America can profit from its example—and avoid its mistakes.

BIRMINGHAM-SOUTHERN:
The Genteel Tradition on a
Southern Campus

Birmingham–Southern College had its frail beginning in 1856 as Southern University in the plantation country of Alabama. Its history was one long financial agony until it merged with Birmingham College in 1918. With the support of Birmingham businessmen, the institution prospered until today it has become one of the leading small colleges in the South. The shift from the embrace of plantation owners to that of steel manufacturers, its gradual transition from a school offering "sanctified education" to a modern "church-related" college—the euphemism is revealing—defines not only Birmingham–Southern's history but that of the South.

The original Methodist founders, fired with zealotry, saw their youth ringed around with perils—"the hotbeds of Calvinism . . . the darkness of Catholic convents . . . the chilling winds of abolitionism . . . the skepticism of state institutions."

"Is it because," a spokesman asked, "we have no Institutions worthy of our patronage? Then let us build them."

They did build them in great profusion. Over the years twelve hundred Methodist schools and colleges went up throughout the young country, most of them far from the temptations of the city.

Those early champions of Methodist probity would be startled at Birmingham–Southern today, where the Newman Society meets with impunity, Baptist and Presbyterian groups enjoy parity with Methodists, and a local rabbi turns up during Religious Emphasis Week. They would look askance at weekly chapels

116

without prayer (down-graded to mere convocations), at beauty contests which churn up more excitement than theology, at heated talk about the Beat Generation in the "Cellar," the local Bohemian retreat. They might recognize the steel magnates as their legitimate successors, but they would still view quizzically the inaugural conference on the "mutuality of business and education."

Nevertheless, BSC is still unmistakably a denominational school —and a Southern one. The Ministerial Association coexists amiably with the Physical Education Club. The president, a Methodist layman, teaches Sunday school—although attired occasionally in silk suit and two-toned shoes. The girls are exemplars of Southern gentility.

Above all, there is a stubborn and coherent consciousness among students and faculty of a Southern tradition, even if its content is gradually thinning out under the onslaught of modernism. The college catalogue refers lugubriously to the "dark days of the sixties," as if it were only yesterday. Southern oratory is fostered by scholarships awarded to high school boys with a talent for the polished utterance. The most popular of the adult education courses deals with the campaigns of the War Between the States. In the library musty portraits of Southern generals look down on as chic a collection of highbrow quarterlies as can be found anywhere. A boy announced to me magisterially that his birthplace was the "Tigris-Euphrates of the South." He said it with a twinkle which hardly belied his proud sense of place.

BSC is located three miles from the business center of Birmingham on 250 acres of high wooded ground. The area is beginning to look seedy. Birmingham, like most cities, has brisk, new suburban developments; to live outside of the industrial valley— "over the mountain"—is an important status symbol. The college, however, presents a neat, attractive spread of eleven buildings, most of them in sober Georgian architecture. At night, from the top of campus hill, students see tongues of flame from the blast furnaces in the valley below.

Many people insist that Birmingham is not really a Southern city—there are far too many steelworkers from the North, and anyway the true South is cotton-rural. That is largely a sentimental pose. Those who showed me around the city apologized for the statue of Vulcan, an ungainly brute fifty-five feet high— the only statue in the country to celebrate industry. But they took a furtive pride in its sheer muscular grotesquerie and were quick to point out that it is second in size only to the Statue of Liberty.

The college has a thousand full-time students, a plant worth $9 million, and a modest $4 million endowment (tuition is only $600 a year, a bargain by any standards.) Its achievements belie its size. Academically, it is very sturdy. It has a Phi Beta Kappa chapter, and only one private college in the South has produced, among its graduates, more Ph.D.'s during the last twenty years. Its living alumni include ten college presidents and twenty-eight deans and administrators. There is one faculty member for each ten to fifteen students, and the staff is well trained (60 per cent Ph.D.'s—a high figure for a Southern school). There is a symbolic appropriateness about the ghostly football stadium, the stands splintery, the field overgrown. ("We were one of the first schools to get out from under," President Henry King Stanford remarked.) It will soon make way for a handsome new arts center.

Largely a commuters' college, only one-third of BSC students live on campus. (Plans for the future include an increase of on-campus students.) Despite the presence of some foreign students, it is essentially a local school, an unhurried backwater, somewhat ingrown, a touch provincial. An instructor of German observed that *"Ich bin hier"* is likely to come out *"Ich bin hee-ah,"* but the director of the college theater has a preference for foreign plays because the students do better imitating foreign tongues than standard American (which, they insist, they have been speaking all along).

BSC is regarded as a "study school" in contrast with the University of Alabama, which is sometimes described as the "country club of the South." A typical attitude is expressed by the student who said, "I wouldn't say that I'm an intellectual, but I like the serious atmosphere." A pretty girl said plaintively: "I was a straight A student in high school back home in Demopolis. I came here and got all B's and C's. I was all tore up."

A fraternity boy remarked, "Study is a norm here. Everybody studies, so it's not hard to do."

The college is on a three-quarter system (three courses a semester, five hours a week for each). This seems to work well for science and mathematics, not so well for the humanities in which time is needed for intellectual gestation. Pre-medical and pre-dental courses are reputed to be the best in the state. For selected students there is available a science major of the most formidable proportions.

At the same time, the college has to fight off pressures toward vocationalism. It divested itself of a weak journalism major, but it still offers secretarial studies for girls, and there are far more courses in business administration (including accounting) than there are in religion. Education courses flourish, particularly for women who are likely to capitulate to their mothers' admonition to provide "*in*surance for the future." Attached to the college is a conservatory of music, and its major role in the life of the institution probably derives from the Southern tradition of the well-brought-up lady. Challenging also is the fact that BSC offers ballet classes but no modern dancing. (Grahamesque contractions and percussive movements are here regarded as neither pretty nor ladylike.) There is some disaffection between science and arts students. It is easy to do well in the humanities, science majors assert, because there are no labs. Literature students counter that outside reading is equivalent to a lab. Science people have to fight the image of themselves as inarticulate troglodytes at ease only with test tubes. "I should never have told my English prof that I'm a science major," a student remarked. "He immediately assumed that I could never interpret a poem." The science faculty argues, with some justice, that they are better informed about the arts than the arts faculty is about the sciences. The humanities people, in turn, titter at the lapses in grammar that occasionally disfigure science brochures.

The college offers an art major and a talented artist-in-residence. Raymond J. MacMahon is a militant abstractionist ("Art is man's invention aimed at changing and improving nature"). "There is no aggressive opposition to modern art," he observed. The trustees, largely other-directed types, dutifully take modern art courses in the evening.

Of course, there are the inevitable threnodies about student listlessness. "Your Brooklyn College students would devour us," a faculty member said enviously to me. A sociology professor observed that Southern students are markedly restrained and non-competitive. He recalls how in his student days in the South if a student left an examination room early, his departure was greeted by the stamping of feet; the folkways had been flouted. Recently, this professor criticized William Graham Sumner's thesis about the ascendency of mores over law. His students, living in one of the chief bastions of segregation, carefully took notes, unmindful of the controversial implications of what they were writing.

I attended an English class concerned with Coleridge's *Biographia Literaria*. The professor, an able scholar, talked about "the sacramental unity of the world apprehended through the imagination." The students exhibited a kind of uneasy reverence for this imposing formulation as, heads bent, they piously took their ration of notes. At one point, the instructor asked, "Does anybody know what happens to poets in Plato's Republic?" No one responded. At the end of the session, crammed with the big issues of literary criticism, he asked hopefully, "Any questions?" There were none.

A psychology professor, active in counseling, sees BSC students as intellectually capable but academically stunted because of the poor quality of high school education in the state, particularly in rural areas. (It is possible to negotiate both high school and college in Alabama without any contact with mathematics.)

The Cellar, however, is pointed to as luminously intellectual. "It's our own existentialist bistro," the president said affectionately. The Cellar is a coffee shop in which the walls are lined with paperbacks, the tables cluttered with coffee cups, and the air is thick with talk—bold, fearless, cosmopolitan talk which vaults the narrow barriers of Jones Valley.

The academic community is divided in its view of the cave dwellers. There is the usual scorn for the sedulous nonconformity of beards, uncombed hair, and shaved heads. A faculty member said sourly, "There's a group here which thinks that if you sit in the Cellar and read the Manchester *Guardian*, you're an intellectual." However, a freshman girl said with awe, "I wouldn't dare go near the Cellar. You've got to be brilliant for them." The

Cellar is under the benign supervision of a lady who sells the paperbacks, dispenses the coffee, and listens to the wild and whirling words with indulgent calm.

It would appear that the South does not provide a congenial atmosphere for rebellion. There is no student iconoclast, for example, like Richard Wheeler at the University of Wisconsin. The *Hilltop New*'s columnist is likely to urge students to be more polite at convocation.

BSC itself has an intimate, familial flavor which dulls the edge of insurgency. There is a pervasive affection, a binding network of relationships that ensnares everybody. The president's wife, for example, takes courses at the college. At a convocation I attended, Dr. Stanford announced genially: "There's someone special in the front row . . . my sweet mother-in-law." The students laughed appreciatively. At the end of the convocation, which featured a piano recital, a dean said of the girls who performed, "They sounded nice, and they looked real pretty." (This sense of ubiquitous family may have a good deal to do with the reluctance of Southern liberals to oppose the values of their community on the race issue.)

When Southern University was planned, the argument advanced in its behalf was that young people sent to college far from home were likely to "imbibe vicious principles." The search for a local habitation with the appropriate trappings of virtue was intense and faintly comic. For a while Auburn was in the lead over Greensboro because there was "no gambling, loafing, or drinking" there. In addition, Southerners can little resist noble literary associations, and Auburn ("loveliest village of the plain") was the hallowed name of Goldsmith's Deserted Village. In the end, both villages won, becoming the sites of Methodist colleges.

The founding fathers triumphed better than they knew, for Priapic stirrings are still effectively contained. A faculty member, attending a fraternity party, was dismayed to find that there were no drinks and that the students were earnestly discussing grades. "When I was at college," he said with some indignation, "it was considered good form for fraternity men to fail their courses."

Certainly in contrast with the aggressive hedonism of the University of Wisconsin, BSC has a thin-lipped gentility. The pleasures of the flesh have only a furtive existence. There is no drinking at all in fraternity houses—there isn't even beer at rush parties. According to one estimate, only about one-quarter of the girls smoke.

"I don't object to girls smoking on moral grounds," a boy said. "I think it's unfeminine."

In the uncharted wilderness of sex, the students of BSC are particularly circumspect. "I attended fraternity conventions and talked to boys from other schools," a young man recalled. "The kind of thing they do is just unheard of here." Men and women alike have a sense of being under stern surveillance. "If a girl has a reputation for being loose and you're seen with her," another fraternity man said, "word gets around. It's like a small Southern town."

The girls openly proclaim their virtue. "I think we stand up for our morals more," a girl said primly. "You know, Northern boys are fascinated by that." And she told of a Harvard boy's bewilderment at her exigent moral code. "If it were known that a girl was having an affair," a sorority member said, "she could hardly exist on campus. It's almost unthinkable."

For many girls college is a reversal of the usual pattern. It brings not a broadening of personal freedom, or an access of sophistication, but rather the restraints imposed by a community of moral peers. High school, with its conglomerate population, was likely to be a good deal more unbuttoned. College turns out to be a kind of "cold convent," as one professor termed it. On the other hand, it is also where received fundamentalist ideas are likely to be eroded.

"The boys are very polite," a coed remarked. "It takes them about five dates to warm up. In high school I had to act like a prude, but not here. Either they can tell by looking at you, or they just don't have it on their mind."

I visited two sororities, where I saw two faces of the South. The Pi Beta Phi's, many of whom are ministers' daughters, call themselves "the Bible-carrying Pi Phi's," and boast of having the highest scholastic index. One of their songs explains that when a Pi Phi goes walking with her one and only man, she won't let him hold her hand, because a Pi Phi is an angel in disguise. "From the time I came here," a Pi Phi in a simple cotton dress explained, "I never smelled liquor on anyone's breath. I'm a Methodist from head to toe."

A girl sang a torchy blues number. The sorority girls and their pledgees stood in a decorous semicircle gravely snapping their fingers. Not a hip was in motion. The beat picked up, and the entertainer's pelvic movements gained in intensity. "She's only a pledgee," a sorority officer whispered to me half in explanation and half in disavowal.

Nevertheless some Pi Phi's protested, "We're human too," and one girl described a foray into the back country in quest of a drinking place:

"There's this little nothing of a place down nowhere. The atmosphere is so different from the college. You turn off on a gravel road, then you swing into a little mud road, and then you go deep into the woods. The place is just a shack. The paint's peeling off the wall, the bulb flickers, and it's cold near the windows." She paused, then added with a delicious shiver, "But the band's real good."

Alpha Omicron Pi, on the other hand, represents a bold slash of sophistication in the magnolia belt. Instead of frilly frocks, some of the girls wore tight toreador pants. There were Picasso prints on the wall and primitive statuary on the shelves. "The Pi Phi's are sweet," an AOPi officer said, "but we're more aggressive, more liberal. We pride ourselves on our individuality." Tolerant about drinking, they expect boys to be moderate about it and to maintain their social standards at all times.

A fraternity boy, a product of the Age of Eisenhower, expressed his preference for "the more liberal of the Pi Phi's and the more conservative of the AOpi's." His brothers nodded their heads in agreement.

Both sororities have in common an exuberant hospitality. "We're so glad you dropped in," they trilled. After the third or fourth time, it was clear that this was merely a conventional utterance. The Southern college girl is soft, respectful, and artfully feminine, in ironic contrast to the remorseless momism of the South.

One of the striking features of life at BSC is the deep bow to feminine beauty. Every issue of the school newspaper has some cautious but worshipful cheesecake. Every fraternity has a sweetheart elected with great fanfare. The grand climax of the school year is the selection of Miss Southern Accent. ("The fifteen finalists will appear in white evening gowns accented by delicate orchid nosegays.") In 1959 it was Margie Mills, a lovely, solemn-faced girl, determinedly unglamorous, with none of the postures of the aspiring starlet. How did she feel about winning?

"It made my mother real proud."

A recent beauty garnered additional laurels as Miss Alabama and as runner-up in the Atlantic City Beauty Contest. (Miss Alabama, through some clever footwork, seems to have become a special province of BSC.) Willie-Lee Thornberry (she has since dropped the Willie as immitigably provincial) went on to New York and a career, hopefully, in show business. The school newspaper avidly reported her appearance on the Dave Garroway Show: She did her numbers ("Honey Bun," "Steam Heat," and "Small Hotel") and then exhibited her baseball-pitching prowess which had "helped the AOPi's in intramurals last year."

Miss Thornberry, in less than a year, modeled dresses in the garment center, had a part in an off-Broadway play, and was in the chorus of an industrial show. "In the garment center," she recalled, "they treated me the way a little Southern belle should be. I told my momma that I was getting worried. Nobody had even propositioned me. She said that I was probably so naive I didn't even know when I was being propositioned."

The thriving theater group, almost one hundred strong, has watched Miss Thornberry's career with proprietary interest. The North to most of them means freedom . . . the opportunity to experiment . . . exotic people. Like theater kids everywhere, the girls wear paint-smeared dungarees, the boys have an air of almost desperate aestheticism, and there is the usual clatter of hammers and saws. The group, eclectic and unafraid, has produced such plays as *Antigone* and *Playboy of the Western World*, as well as such lightweight staples as *Harvey*. A few years ago they presented *The World of Sholom Aleichem* with the help of people in the community, the Southern drawl temporarily crossed with a Yiddish accent. The leads, providentially, were played by

Jewish members of the community. But a comic incongruity, recalled by the director, was "the presence in this very Jewish haven of a typically Nordic blonde angel named Hildegarde Spears."

The chumminess of college and community extends to other areas as well. It was explained to me that Birmingham is actually like a small Southern town. Strip away the working-class component, which is large, and the Negro community with which there is no contact, and what is left is a small cultural elite. ("Do you know J. D. Salinger?" someone asked me, projecting his own experience of a small literary coterie onto the vast literary subcontinent of New York City.)

The Birmingham Civic Ballet Company, one of the best community groups in the country, would be helpless without BSC students. "We're not hothouse flowers," a college student in the company remarked. "We're a contributing part of the city. We realize that there is a world outside of ballet." For local businessmen, it was a jolt to discover that the ballet company, originally something of a joke, was getting more publicity than the steel mills. They learned their lesson: today, half the audience at a ballet performance consists of men.

In the old days BSC was a "preachers' college." Daily chapel was mandatory, and the atmosphere was fiercely sacerdotal. Today, one-eighth of the students are preparing for full-time Christian work. (Many of the women will never make it; they will marry ministers en route.) Some students have weekend pastorates. Sons of ordained clergy get a moderate reduction in tuition fees. Nevertheless, Birmingham–Southern's denominationalism has a modern liberal complexion.

"Here we look at various interpretations of the religious life," a member of the Religion Department stated. "My approach is in the Kantian tradition . . . that the heart of religion is ethics. You might say that our goal is an ethically-oriented theism."

He would like to see the college ally itself to the more progressive elements of the Methodist Church. In any case, he asserted, the tone of BSC is far healthier than the "aggressive secularism" of the state schools.

President Stanford, in acknowledging an obligation to the

church, pointed out that spiritual values can be achieved in many ways. A graduate student told him that the strongest spiritual influence he encountered at BSC was a professor of chemistry with a firm commitment to a moral order in the universe. There is a greater interest in religion today than there was twenty years ago and on a much more sophisticated level.

"When I was a student here," a faculty member recalled, "a boy might be disturbed by the theory of evolution. Now most of our students have resolved that problem in high school."

Both students and faculty have a patronizing attitude toward Howard College, a large Baptist school just outside of town. One professor at BSC sees Howard as "mass-producers of ministers and teachers," and its students as raw bumpkins "who have never been further than the barn." Nor does the pious atmosphere at Howard inspire much respect.

"They pray around a tree over there," a student said maliciously, "and there are signs all over the place saying, 'Have you prayed today?' "

An administrator at BSC reported with some dismay that Howard College, in settling on a new campus, built from scratch and erected conventional red brick Georgian buildings. "What a pity! They could have done anything they wanted," he said, his eyes aglow with visions of riotous avant-gardism.

BSC's liberalism expresses itself in providing a haven for the Newman Society as well as for non-Methodist Protestant groups. There are a few Jewish students on campus as well, and it is characteristic of the warm, familial flavor that Jewish students are reluctant to create issues about social exclusion.

"I knew that some of the fraternities couldn't pledge me, while others could," a young man explained. "I decided that I wouldn't pledge at all in order not to embarrass anyone."

Alabama's Birmingham–Southern College is torn between a stubborn regional loyalty and the lure of the sophisticated North. It offers a series of lectures by Distinguished Southern Professors (one of whom is from New Jersey), but the Rushton Lecturers have included such luminaries from the great world as Arnold Toynbee, Howard Memford Jones, Karl Compton, and Francis Henry Taylor. Among its visiting professors have been such Ivy

League notables as Harry Carman of Columbia, Henri Peyre of Yale, and Willard Thorp of Princeton. BSC gallantly sends some of its political science majors for a semester to that only vaguely Southern city, Washington, D.C., to catch a glimpse of government in action.

Southernism dies hard. It is part rhetoric, part romantic legend, and part thumbing of the nose at the rich, smug North. A fraternity boy talked with pride of seeing an original Ku Klux Klan uniform hanging in his grandfather's closet ("The current Ku Klux doesn't deserve to be mentioned in the same breath"). President Stanford lovingly quotes his granduncle who used to say, "We didn't lose the war; we wore ourselves out whipping the Yankees!"

Southern pique at the facile snobberies of the North was expressed by a boy who declared: "When my high school graduating class came to New York, we discovered that Northerners expected us to be barefoot. So we took our shoes off and put our feet out the window of the bus."

But there is also a sense among BSC students that the mystique of the South verges on absurdity. There is always an element of sly burlesque when the Southerner is most Southern. A Confederate flag was flown by a fraternity on Lee's birthday. A wag in a rival fraternity climbed atop an adjoining building and sent a flaming arrow into the flag. A newspaper in town published an account of the desecration, and the local chapter of United Daughters of the Confederacy howled.

The South, like New England, has a fondness for its home-bred eccentricities. Faculty members talked with amusement about former President Guy E. Snavely, now the chancellor. His disapproval of smoking is so thunderous that professors have been known to stub out cigarettes in the palm of their hands when he turns up unexpectedly. He once stopped a young faculty member, handed him a sheet of paper, and said imperiously, "Boy, send off this telegram!"

BSC students and faculty are largely gradualists, with a sprinkling of integrationists, and some old-fashioned fire-eating segregationists. But the issue, crucial as it is, seems to provoke more exasperation than troubled concern.

"Northerners are much more interested in integration than we are," a student remarked. "It's the first thing they talk about when they come down here."

He was startled to learn that Rev. Martin Luther King who was then in Montgomery, has heroic dimensions in the North.

The prevailing attitude is one of uneasy standpattism. A not untypical attitude was conveyed by a pre-ministerial student: "In a Christian idealistic way, I am for integration. But on the practical level, I am against it. The Negro is in a lower socioeconomic group, and you can't mix with him."

A student leader said thoughtfully: "Intelligent Southerners have gotten over the idea that Negroes are descendants of Ham. Old ideas of racial superiority are going. However, Southerners feel that people in the North have this superior moral attitude. They don't really understand the situation here." Another student shifted the moral burden by saying, "The Yankee traders brought the slaves in, and you can't legislate social differences out." A candid boy said, "Integration doesn't bother me, but I don't want them to stop doing for us."

A lone voice crying out in the wasteland of prudence is that of Tommy Reeves, a BSC student and part-time minister, who was banished by threats of violence from his rural pastorate because of his views on integration. He said earnestly, "Gradualism doesn't obscure the need to do something now. In Birmingham schools it's prohibited to discuss race problems. It's a terrible thing when you can't educate people to love."

Shortly before graduation, Reeves was arrested by the local police on a charge of vagrancy. For eighteen hours no one at the college was permitted to see him. He received his degree on schedule despite protests from the Ku Klux Klan and White Citizens' Council. The charge against him was dropped by the police the day after graduation.

The college itself likes the idea of a strong moral commitment on the part of its students, but it is also cautious. It wants to become a first-class institution, and, as an administrator remarked, "You can't get too far ahead of your constituency." Birmingham is a center of rabid, strong-arm racism, and most people of good will there have been cowed. There was real eloquence in the gesture of one of the faculty who, soon after I arrived in Birmingham, drove me through a handsome Negro suburban development, full of beautifully maintained ranch houses. (The income of Negroes in Birmingham is among the highest of their race in the South; more than half the Negro families own their own homes.) But this display of Negro opulence only heightened the pathos of the voicelessness which separates middle-class white and middle-class Negro.

The faculty at Birmingham–Southern is pleasant, amiably argumentative, and intellectually alert. "There are few goofers here," a recent addition observed. "I go into the lunchroom, and there's always a lively exchange among people from various disciplines."

Salaries are modest but no lower than in many schools of its size. With the help of foundations, the average for full professor is $7,140 (with a top salary of $8,600 after twenty-two years); for associate professor, $5,783; for assistant professor, $4,804; for instructor, $3,800. (There are relatively few instructors because of the inflationary spiral in personnel recruitment.) Any appraisal of salary has to take into account the housing arrangement on Greensboro Road, where, with loans made by the college, a member of the faculty can build well and inexpensively.

Recruitment of good people in these days of educational panic is increasingly difficult. In scarcity fields, such as the sciences, relatively young men are brought in as associate professors. This generates resentment in less pinched departments where "there are some right good people around." And every year, there is the tense drama of how many people will be snatched away by marauding colleges dangling rank and money in seductive fashion. In the last few years, a history man became dean of Washington and Lee, while another became chairman of the history department at the University of Georgia. This year a psychology professor was lured to the University of South Florida.

BSC has a teaching faculty rather than a research one. The normal teaching load is fifteen hours, a heavy burden which relieves the faculty of any stern obligation to publish. This may very well be unwholesome. There is reason to believe that more members of the faculty would engage in scholarly activity if pressure were applied. But life for the faculty is probably pleasanter at BSC than at a large university with its cutthroat competition and steady pressures. There is even more scope for a leisurely and dilettante (in the good sense) life of the mind, since there is less urgency to burrow in one's narrow little specialization.

There are also particular virtues in teaching in a small, fluid, unstratified school like BSC. A French professor reported that when there was demand for only two courses in his field, he introduced a course in Dante and one in Russian literature in translation. The intellectual quickening which this afforded is incalculable. "At the University of North Carolina," he pointed out, "I would have to wait for the Dante man to die." On the other hand, in many of the smaller departments—philosophy and sociology, for example—there is only one teacher with the inevitable loss of that vital cross-fertilization of ideas that comes from having someone else to talk to.

Many windows are kept open on the world of scholarship. With the help of foundation money, the staff gets around to conventions, meetings, and on private research junkets. (The ivory tower has become highly mobile. College professors these days do a great deal of traveling. On a tight salary, life at home may be grubby, but on expense-paid trips, the living is easier.) At BSC the faculty is more inclined to attend Southern regional meetings of scholarly organizations than national conventions, but the Mason and Dixon line is often breached. However, these jaunts into the world outside sometimes exacerbate feelings of inferiority vis-à-vis the North.

Otherwise, life for the faculty is ingrown—they teach next door to each other in Munger or Phillips Hall and then peer at each other over the split-rail fence on Greensboro Road. Dinner parties are the staple entertainment, and, as one faculty wife said, "The art of gossip is kept alive." College politics are held in check by a Southern sense of decorum. Moreover, the school is so small, the president so accessible, that the paranoiac we-they view of the administrative apparatus is hard to maintain.

There are some minor skirmishes over smoking and drinking. In the old days faculty could smoke only beyond the college rail. Today the drinkers and smokers outnumber the abstainers. But the fundamentalist ethos dies hard. I attended a dinner party given by a member of the faculty, where cocktails were served. A professor who had promised to show me around a college dance asked me if I still wanted to go.

"You see," he explained, "if I have to go to the dance I can't drink. But if I'm not going, I can have a cocktail or two."

Faculty row is like a small suburban development—the neatly spaced homes getting more contemporary in design the further down (the lower in rank and age) you go; the carports and the tow-headed children more numerous. Life on a tight budget is reasonably tranquil.

"During the thirties," a professor with a long memory recalled, "there was lots of worrying about Loyalist Spain. Today the faculty is interested in payments on the washing machine and changes in the pension plan."

Sometimes they are interested in each other. A recent arrival, a gifted teacher with a solemn respect for his own crochets, has provoked a good deal of talk, much of it good-natured. This man has been known to have wine parties-cum-discussions with his students. Tame stuff at Harvard, it is bold adventuring at BSC. His home, in particular, has generated furious gossip. A crisis developed when he presented plans for an ultramodern dwelling, charitably described as "a boxcar turned over." The president had a tough decision to make: Should the college impose its tastes on the new faculty member? In the end, the professor's academic prowess won him immunity for his architectural venturesomeness. However, the academic lanes buzzed with indignation anew when his laundry was unfurled defiantly on the front lawn. (The terrain drops sharply in back of his house where clothes lines are normally strung.) He has since acquired a clothes dryer, but on sunny days the laundry bravely reappears.

"The idea of going to Birmingham–Southern threw me at first," a faculty member said. "Then people where I was teaching began to say nice things about it, and I decided to come. It's an odd situation. We have a nice administration and good students, but we're in Birmingham—a cultural fortress surrounded by a wilderness."

Another professor feels stifled by the all-enveloping decorum.

"You don't get the occasional wild woman here you find on other campuses," he observed. "I know they upset things, but they add color—you know, the kind who dresses as if she doesn't care what people think, or who dedicates herself passionately to English madrigals."

The race problem creates a brooding disquietude. Most of BSC's faculty is Southern. The dangers of provincialism are apparent to all. But as long as vast areas of the South are subservient to the White Citizens' Councils, it will be difficult to attract able academicians from the North. A professor at the University of Wisconsin said angrily, "Why should I send graduate students to teach in the South and subject them to what's going on there?"

At BSC a man from the North told me uneasily that his young son had pointed to a Negro and said, "I don't like him. He's black." The wife of this professor had become friendly with a Negro woman, a college graduate with whom she worked. When they socialized on Greensboro Road, it was indicated to her that one doesn't do such things. She had to resort to the grotesque subterfuge of hiring the woman as a baby sitter in order to maintain contact.

Dr. Henry King Stanford is that rare phenomenon—a popular college president. Like Birmingham–Southern itself, he represents the mingling of the old and new. Courtly and graceful, he has a sympathetic appreciation of the Southern tradition, but he is shrewdly attuned to current realities. Moreover, he has had his fling beyond the sacred groves. He received his Ph.D. in political science from New York University, worked for a time with the National Association of Manufacturers, and did a stint in Turkey with a government mission. And he is young, slightly over forty. His description of the faculty—"Southern but urbane"—applies with particular force to him. He drives a gleaming new Cadillac ("one of the advantages of having rich trustees"), dresses jauntily, and has a lively though civilized sense of life's spoils. The day I arrived I was taken to dinner by Dr. Stanford at a private hilltop dining club called with panache "The Club." (It is inevitable that a peevish member of the faculty would complain about this: "Stanford tries to show his sophistication," he said. "You know, he'll say, 'Yes, you do use vodka in a screwdriver.' ")

Skillful in his relations with the college's benefactors, yet genuinely responsive to ideas, Stanford has won a secure place in his short tenure. There is some anxiety that he will be snapped up by a larger institution and then replaced by "some little old Methodist preacher." In fact, in the spring of 1960 he was one of a distinguished group of candidates considered for the chancellorship of the municipal colleges of New York City.

He defined the function of BSC as "a kind of academic conscience for the community." Like college presidents everywhere, Stanford is driving hard toward excellence. Private colleges should be dedicated to quality, he argues. On the other hand, he does not envision Birmingham–Southern merely as a breeding ground for Phi Beta Kappa's.

"We want a good sprinkling of C students," he said. "They're the ones who go on to make the money with which to endow our college in the future."

BSC has an amicable rivalry with Agnes Scott, Davidson, University of the South, Southwestern at Memphis, and Randolph–Macon. But excellence in this league is not enough, Stanford asserts. "We should now lift our sights to national standards of excellence and exert every effort to achieve them," he declared at his inauguration. A student speaker on the same occasion touched on another reality: "This hilltop rises above a valley shadowed by fears and ignorance. . . . The people of the earth look to such institutions as Birmingham–Southern college for guidance."

There are intimations that the college is beginning to respond to current challenges. A student editorial recently assailed the states' rights issue as "a disguise used by certain people to cover their childish prejudices." The editorialist then asked soberly: "Do you want the South continually to be degraded and to rot in illiteracy? If you do, states' rights will certainly do it. But if you want to revive the South, then do away with your prejudices and antiquated opinions such as states' rights. Only then can the South rise to greatness."

In the spring of 1960, ninety-seven BSC students sent a petition to Governor Patterson of Alabama protesting the expulsion of nine Negro students from Alabama State College for their role in lunchroom sit-in demonstrations. When pressed for comment, Dr. Stanford reaffirmed the constitutional right of students to petition and underlined the traditional college policy of respecting freedom of expression. "It is a sad day for our country," he added, "whenever the exercise of these freedoms has to be explained or defended." Dr. Stanford's response was neatly reproachful, yet it did not invite destructive antagonism. Birmingham–Southern College may yet offer the guidance for which many of its earnest students, caught between an elevated Christian morality and an inherited racism, yearn.

For Ladies Mostly

SMITH: The College for All-Around Girls

Smith College is imposingly one of the Big Seven, **the** very archetype of the good women's college. The largest of its type, it mediates between the artistic ardors of Sarah Lawrence on the one hand and the austere bookishness of Bryn Mawr on the other. But it is uniquely itself, too, and the core of its *persona* is a commitment to purposeful activity, energy, health. The Smith girl was an Organization Woman long before the term became pejorative. And the standing joke concerns four alumnae who meet accidentally, and, before you know it, have elected a president, vice-president, secretary, and treasurer.

At Smith the All-American girl—upper-class style—is apotheosized and trained. She emerges fully accoutered to rout the forces of darkness in the suburban community in which she will ultimately settle. At the least, Smith offers basic training for PTA chairmanship. But there are loftier reaches too: Smith women are deployed all over the world as helpmeets for successful and influential husbands, and as shakers and movers in their own right. An awe-struck member of the faculty said reverently: "The Smith girl is the kind who winds up administering a museum, two hospitals, and serving as a trustee with the Boston Symphony."

Little more than eighty-five years old, Smith projects a sense of being a venerable institution with a long-established ethos—like Harvard's—that students and faculty can flout only at the risk of standing in the cold and dark outside the True Church. That ethos is compounded of a commitment to work Spartan in its rigor; a sense of noblesse oblige, which sends its students pellmell to political meeting, settlement house, and even picket line; and habits of play which are part of the life-style of the upper-class

American. Aristocratic in its origins, Smith has incorporated the cautious egalitarianism of our time.

The result is a bubbling cauldron of opposites. The Smith student, a faculty member remarked, is a combination of Peck and Peck and Quaker simplicity. (Resolving the antinomies in the Smith psyche is a favorite indoor sport of the faculty during long winter evenings.) Another professor had a vision of the inner reality of Smith in terms of a double page in *The New York Times* Magazine. On one page his mind's eye saw a dour analysis of the judicial process with a grim title like "The Agony of Duty." On the other page, there is a chic ad for a new fabric, showing an elegant lady with a Negro slave, bearing flowers, crouching at her feet and looking up adoringly at her. Any Smith College bulletin board will offer polarities almost as gaudy. On one board a sign gaily tantalized: "Bermuda College Week. Ten glorious days at beautiful Sunny Isle Cottages." Another poster, in far more hortatory mood, announced: "Weekend work camp. Understand the problems of living in a hard-hit urban area. Help by working a full-day painting, wall-papering, cleaning up, fixing up with a Roxbury family and other campers."

Both sides are Smith—bridge table and unflinching solitary labor in the Libe (Library); weekends at Yale and arduous study for "writtens"; a quick run to Switzerland for skiing over Christmas and the boycott of a local store for overcharging. The typical Smith girl, a political science professor summarized, is likely to be the liberal daughter of a staunch Republican father.

In a way that is uniquely America in mid-century, Smith reflects ease and accommodation—the goals of suburbia triumphant —and underneath a nagging disquietude about the flaccidity of life. No student body anywhere agonizes as much about the perils of conformity.

Smith College has 2,200 students and a faculty of 230. It offers 312 courses in 29 departments, including 12 interdepartmental courses. Its library, with over 400,000 volumes, is the largest of any women's college and prepossessing by any standards. It is essentially a traditional school concerned with the liberal arts— women's colleges can afford to be nonvocational. It has a big honors program, which means, of course, independent study; a junior year abroad; and, in the fashion of most good schools to-day, it zealously scouts developments on other campuses and does a fair share of academic introspection. Nestled in the Connecticut River Valley, 150 miles northwest of New York, it has joined three local schools—Mount Holyoke, Amherst, and the University of Massachusetts—in a system of planned academic cooperation (some joint classes, pooled library resources, common cultural activities).

The college itself is two hundred acres of verdant meadow, sparkling pond—called without self-consciousness Paradise Pond —and a wild mélange of buildings cast in Georgian, Romanesque, Greek Revival, and Gothic styles—"factory Gothic," one professor said scornfully. Recently two modern dormitories—an aggressive thrust of glass and brick—have appeared. Over-all, the campus has a kind of dingy charm, reminders of the past are everywhere (including an old-fashioned gong which announces the end of class), and in the ruins of a torn-down classroom building a whimsical student did pseudoprimitive line paintings of nudes and animals as in some remote Cro-Magnon cave.

There are gaunt reminders of life's perils all around the campus. Paradise Pond has an unparadisical hazard in the form of a small waterfall. A decaying factory building adjoins one end of the campus, and a state mental institution—Dippy House the girls call it—adjoins another.

Smith College opened its doors to fourteen students in 1875, established as the result of a bequest by a generous maiden lady, Sophia Smith of Hatfield, Massachussetts. Finding herself encumbered by a tidy fortune left by her brother, this proper New Englander consulted her minister, who advised her to use the funds for higher education for women. Her will, couched in the homely language of the period, starts with some conventional bequests ("I give and bequeath to my cousins Electa Graves and Charlotte W. Billings, One Thousand Dollars each, and my jewelry, wardrobe, and household furniture, except the large portrait of myself"). Gently feminist Miss Smith then left $400,-000 to found a college "for the higher education of young women, with the design to furnish for my own sex means and facilities for education equal to those which are afforded now in our colleges for young men." That wish has been fulfilled abundantly.

Smith College is expensive, but its annual $2,200 cost (tuition and board) is not higher than that of most first-rate schools. About 20 per cent of the cost of educating its students is borne by the College, which engages in the breakneck fund raising typical of American colleges everywhere. (But the job is tougher for women's colleges, for though women assertedly control the national purse strings, male chauvinism triumphs: the big money goes to men's schools.) Twenty per cent of Smith's students are on scholarship; 35 per cent receive some financial help. Summers about half the girls work. A waitress who earned $1,200 was the highest paid in the summer of 1959.

English, not unexpectedly, is the most popular major, with history second, and art close behind. (A tradition-oriented school, art history and appreciation have ascendency over the creation of new art.) The performing arts have only a modest place in the curriculum. The sciences, heretofore neglected, are beginning to move up in popularity.

Like Harvard, Smith has distribution (prescribed courses in a variety of areas) and concentration (major field) requirements. Like Harvard, too, there is a reading period when the student—presumably liberated from the tyranny of assignments and term papers—can read in depth. In practice, however, the academic pressures are so stringent that the reading period is simply catching-up time.

Smith chooses its girls fastidiously (three are rejected for each one accepted). The Admissions Board looks for all-around girls but eschews "indiscriminate joiners." And fearful of a community of top sergeants, the college professes to be interested in "cooperative followers" as well as in leaders.

What are Smith girls like? For the first time recently more than half have attended public high schools. About 20 per cent are the daughters of alumnae. The girls are garbed in the fashion of their time and place. In winter, long floppy scarves are mandatory; in spring, Bermuda shorts. For a time kilts were the order of the day. The level of pulchritude is more that of Radcliffe than of Sarah Lawrence: lots of short-haired, bookish-looking types but also many stunners with magnificent legs often bared to wintry winds.

Bicycles are ubiquitous—thickets of them all over campus—and on weekends one can see an occasional girl in high heels and cocktail gown astride her vehicle. Even in violent rainstorms the girls still pedal furiously in bulky raincoat and floppy hat, the water cascading from their garments. But stop one in the rain and ask for directions, and she will smile and patiently explain showing those marvelous teeth which seem to gleam brighter at Smith than anywhere else. As at most girls' schools, during the week there is almost total sartorial collapse followed by weekend primping. In their Saturday morning classes, the girls display well-coiffed heads in preparation for their evening dates. The page-boy coiffure, passé elsewhere, still prevails at Smith.

The dominant impression a visitor has is of some fabled country of the young. One sees only hordes of girls spilling from building and dorm—hundreds of them everywhere—and most, with sparkling complexions and trim lines, looking like Miss Rheingold with brains.

An early catalogue of Smith College declared: "It is the wish of the trustees that the young women may also attain a social refinement and culture which will enable them to feel at home in good society. . . ." Politesse of the most exigent kind is still the hallmark of the Smith girl. In fact, visiting lecturers are so politely received that they can hardly appraise their own effectiveness. Local hands, however, can judge from the *kind* of applause how the girls are *really* responding. In the library I saw a student weeping inconsolably. Hovering over her was a sympathetic librarian. Suddenly the girl saw visitors approaching. And through the screen of tears, there burst the dazzling Smith smile.

They are incorrigibly addicted to song. The campus swarms with choral groups including one which even junkets abroad. When President Mendenhall was preparing to leave for Europe not long ago, he was serenaded by two groups. And when Miss Doris Silbert of the Music Department came to class after being named dean (the old title was "warden"), her students sang their congratulations on the spot.

Mary Ellen Chase, novelist and member of Smith's English Department, defined Smith as "a quite unsheltered community of some 2,500 students, some teaching and some being taught, all, let us hope, studying and thinking together." A professorial exile from Smith, however, said sourly, "It was like being in a balloon six miles up." Other Northampton sojourners have dwelled unlovingly on the sense of isolation, heightened—oddly enough in our time of shrinking distances—by the decline in railroad service. (The drive to New York is fatiguing, and there is no convenient plane service.) Girls talk about the "shut-in, inland feeling" that makes them flee on weekends. "But once you come back," a student explained, "the place closes in on you, and it's as if you've never been away." A female professor summed up learnedly, "The microcosm becomes the macrocosm."

Paradoxically, however, Smith is highly cosmopolitan, despite its valley claustrophobia. The faculty abounds with Europeans, and there is frequent contact with the staff of the other three schools in the Four College Plan, as well as lots of lively interchange within the Smith faculty. Columbia University is more insular than Smith, a professor argued, for there you restrict your contacts to your own department. And as a symbol of its leap beyond the New England hills, the Faculty Club has an international cuisine. ("Yes," a wise guy professor said sourly, "they louse everything up with garlic.") Moreover, sooner or late, the world's most distinguished minds make a one-night stand at Smith. Recent visiting personalities included Dean Acheson, Paul Tillich, Harold Taylor, Norman Thomas—as well as Swedish gymnasts and Hindu dancers.

Many faculty members sing the joys of rural living, and they cheerfully endure the quasi-isolation that it may impose. "New York has a ghastly, destructive quality," artist Leonard Baskin remarked. "I go there to be dipped in it, then come back to be cleansed."

Smith's very isolation, in fact, may be responsible for the students' workhorse proclivities. Faculty members are fulsome in their approval. Some point to the girls' stoic endurance of academic burdens. "If the assignment sheet has a 'typo' and calls for three hundred pages overnight instead of thirty, they'll do it," a government professor insisted.

"We're dealing with girls with a higher IQ than that of most college professors," a partisan in the History Department argued. Visitors to the campus are often similarly impressed. Justice Felix Frankfurter gave a talk on the judicial process at Smith. One girl questioned him persistently, trying to pin him down about due process. Half in irritation and half in admiration, he turned to the people on the platform and said grimly, "She's a hanging judge, isn't she?"

If feminism is muted these days among women students, it is rampant among their teachers. Smith professors view their students with a kind of exasperated admiration. They respect the girls' skills and commitment to work, but they are deeply offended by their tendency to sell themselves short and settle for the drab goals of husband and ranch house. With little provocation, the faculty will trumpet the virtues of the self-effacing master race of Smithies and summarily dismiss the claims for excellence of the intellectual serfs at Dartmouth and Amherst.

They contemplate ruefully the low percentage of Smith students who do graduate work (it's part of their class life-style *not* to do graduate work), and their failure to make a mark in the world commensurate with their gifts.

Many observers take the view that though the girls work hard, there is something dogged and joyless about it. Moreover, a sharp line is often drawn between Smith's strenuous academicism and the intellectual life, which, allegedly, has only a fugitive existence on campus. "It's the effect of the kind of mandarins they have here," a mildly rebellious young professor remarked.

"They study hard and they suffer so," a renegade Smithy who transferred to Sarah Lawrence observed. "They take no pleasure in their work. That's why they run off to Yale on weekends. And they don't connect the academic with their lives."

Elizabeth Drew, the distinguished British critic now teaching at Smith, acknowledged that her students rarely read the intellectual quarterlies. "They work hard," she explained, "and they read those glossy magazines to relax. But then, I read detective stories."

Ivy League restraint may be a factor in the attenuation of the intellectual life. "If you have a mink coat, you're apologetic about it," a girl explained. "In the same way, if you have ideas you don't display them." Moreover, there is a fear of spurious intellectualism. "You don't sit in three inches of sawdust and try to define truth," a student said tartly.

The girls glory in their academic hair shirts. A student in a novel course reported that she reads a huge novel a week ("Then you go to class and race to take notes"). A history major said, "There are these lists and lists and lists. And then there's another list with recommended readings. But the titles look enormously interesting, so you read them too."

An honors student reported, with a gasp of incredulity, that last year she did thirty-two papers of more than ten pages each —an average of more than one a week.

I attended an English class and saw again what I had previously observed at Sarah Lawrence: row after row of gray-sweatered girls sitting in respectful passivity. Answers were given softly, almost reverently. Whatever the intellectual stirrings, they were held in check by politesse.

The instructor read and interpreted a Shakespearean sonnet. No one challenged the strategy of the interpretation. When I asked him about the girls' intellectual complaisance, he remarked: "They save their aggressions for their papers. In class they're so passive I could scream. Then they'll do a paper and take a very independent position. Bright boys, in contrast, feel the need to talk far more than bright girls. On the other hand, dull girls don't talk as much as dull boys—and that's a relief. We're free here from the type of bully who usurps lots of class time."

The girls rise spiritedly to their own defense. When compared invidiously with a vocal and enterprising Amherst boy who attends one of her classes, a girl said, "But we *think* before we talk!"

Certainly, the lack of intellectual derring-do derives from their goals, which are tamely predictable. A sociologist on campus distributed a questionnaire to find out what the girls want for themselves in ten years. Theirs is the limited dream of marriage and two or three children—their dissident energies expressing themselves only in token resistance to the standard clubwoman image. After the suburban staples of happiness, they yearn for travel, cultural activity, and a vocation in reserve. (One ingenuous thing wrote merely, "Would like to be married to a Princeton graduate.") The sociology professor concluded sadly, "Nobody wanted to go to the moon. Nobody even wanted to be a millionaire." He described these findings at a faculty dinner party. His colleagues, Smith chauvinists to the end, ganged up on him as a man of doubtful scientific probity and even more doubtful loyalty.

But his image of Smith was confirmed by Mary Ellen Chase, who wrote: "I think few, if any, of us indulge ourselves in the fantastic notions that we shall reform American society, or develop countless masterminds, or turn out many giantesses in the earth. We are, instead, inclined to look upon such presumption as a bit ridiculous, and, on the whole, mistrust taking ourselves too seriously."

As one would expect, Bohemianism, except as a sartorial fling in black stockings and shaggy sweater, does not attract Smith girls. An editorial in *The Sophian*, the student newspaper, glared balefully at the Beat Generation: "Maybe we're too busy following our well-chartered [*sic*] plan of action which includes school, a summer job, dating, reading some very good books, and trying to be 'all-around' people. Who can find time, in the midst of this, to be 'Beat'?"

The "house" system is sometimes alleged to be the source of intellectual drowsiness on campus. On the face of things, the thirty-six houses would seem to be a wholesome idea. They are small—the largest has only eighty-five students—and thus take the curse off impersonal dorm living. They have some of the virtues of sorority life—the groupiness, the ritualized fun—without its nasty snobbishness; everybody, after all, lives in a house at Smith, and students are shuffled around with a view towards heterogeneity in the houses. Each girl is even required to put in a few hours of work weekly—waiting on tables, giving out linen ("Head of Clean Sheets"), retrieving articles left in the living rooms ("Head of Pound"), or holding down the front desk ("on watch"). There is even a proud individualism about the houses.

One house sings at grace, another has a medieval dinner once a year, still another—the smallest of the lot with only sixteen girls —boasts about having a *natural* double octet.

Nevertheless, despite this diversity, the houses bear the brunt of criticism about Smith's flat and gray landscape. A male professor said harshly, "Life in the houses is, on the whole, too country-clubbish, too much emphasis on gracious living."

A student insurgent remarked, "It seems nice at first to have demitasse, and then you wonder, 'What right does a house have to govern the way you dress?'" But even her insurgency had Smithian overtones. She kept saying "sir" to me as deferentially as any proper Smithie ("It's easier to argue with someone when you call him 'sir,'" she explained), and she was utterly dismissive of the Beats ("They're not capable of coping with things like going to the grocery").

The houses have been criticized, too, for the honor system. Social infractions (such as coming in after curfew) *may* be reported by another student, but academic violations (such as plagiarism of cheating) *must* be reported by other students. And some disgruntled girls have described the housemothers as agents of a pervasive spy system. The over-all complaint is that the free life of the mind is suffocated by this tight mesh of arrangements.

A corrosive sketch of Smith was provided by a sharp-eyed Brooklyn College senior who spent a weekend at Northampton. "Everyone looks well scrubbed, blonde, and shiny nosed: powder, rouge, and eyeshadow haven't hit New England yet," she wrote. But this pastorale ends abruptly, she explained, when the girls drink ("When they get 'bombed,' they're uproariously earthy"). As for gracious living, all it means is that "by the time the peas get around to you, they're cold." Her conclusion: "The homogeneity at Smith is just as strong as at Brooklyn College, and the difference in type is just as unimportant as it is uninteresting."

A faculty member had a similar image of the Smith girls: "I sometimes imagine that I see these girls on a conveyor belt which shuffles them through four years of college, through the halls of Seelye [main classroom building] and the library stacks, then on to the altar and kitchen." One girl saw the problem as basically that of admissions. "Smith takes in well-rounded girls," she said, "rather than arty ones who might run off to Mexico in the middle of the semester."

The girls themselves say little to counteract this portrait. A girl described her initial resistance to the modish verbal currency on campus. She bristled every time she heard "Isn't this dear?" and other familiar tags. However, having been bloodied in her mild guerrilla warfare, she finally went out and bought a camel's-hair coat as a gesture of filial submission.

A few years ago, a bright and bratty Harvard *Crimson* boy cased Smith over a weekend and found it hopelessly middle-class, social rather than intellectual, and aggressively wholesome ("Jack Kerouac wouldn't stand a chance"). The response in the student newspaper was one of rueful assent to this portrait, except for one girl who insisted that Smith is upperclass ("Their very attire denotes upper-class conservatism, upper-class security").

Not uncharacteristically, Smith girls have tried to do something about their intellectual pallor by *organizing* intellectual activity on campus. In the spring, there is a week-long arts festival with every house out on a cultural bender: concerts, play-readings, discussions, dance recitals, and art exhibits. (Also characteristic was one tent at the art exhibit labeled forlornly "Salon of the Rejected.") And at least one house has instituted a cultural hour after dinner instead of the usual bridge game.

But no matter which way the intellectual winds blow, the social wheels go round as dizzily as anywhere else—but with one significant difference: midweek the campus is denuded of males. On weekends, of course, the Campfire Girls are transformed into charmers in black sheaths. "It's unnatural," a girl complained. "It always has to be a big deal. There's no casual sitting over a cup of coffee. Then there's the big fuss about going away. And because you're going away you have to study all week, so midweek the place is gloomy."

There are some local male resources, but these are generally slighted in favor of stock more deeply steeped in Ivy. New Haven is downriver, Dartmouth is up. The girls go to both places, and Yalies and Dartmouth men are washed ashore on Friday or

Saturday. It's one of the rituals of Dartmouth—the home of the stout-muscled—to paddle the 150 miles down from Hanover in the spring.

Amherst boys are somewhat derogated—"convenient but junior Ivy League." As for the University of Massachusetts stock, despite the girls' avowals of democracy, they are generally ignored by the class-conscious Smithies.

Social life starts out with a roar. "In freshman year, you're just swept off your feet," a girl remarked. "It's all weekends and rushing off to football games." In freshman year, another worldling explained, the girls try too hard, talk too loud, drink more than they really want to. Later on, they relax and do simple things like taking a walk.

Junior year seems to be the Great Divide. The edge wears off the social frenzy. The girls feel too old for Amherst boys, and running off weekends seems like too much trouble. Moreover, as upperclassmen they become more inward, quieter, and study harder. Academic life becomes more satisfying at precisely the time that their social lives begin to contract—at least on the college fun level.

The upperclassmen look wistfully at the grownup joys of Radcliffe, where there is an inexhaustible stockpile of older graduate students, and where social life reputedly is free from undergraduate fatuities.

President Mendenhall is alert to the dangers of the weekend syndrome, and in promoting the Four College Plan he hopes that it will help keep the girls at home. In his first chapel talk, he said somberly: "Here we have the opportunity to learn, or to recapture, the friendly pleasures of living in a small town, with a still-unspoiled countryside at our door. One of the things I would most wish for you is that you may learn to appreciate and enjoy all this and not flee too carelessly or continually seeking other pastures, perhaps differently populated, but not really greener."

There is no hysteria about getting married—just a steady, relentless pressure. In a recent senior class, only ten girls out of five hundred were married. Many, to be sure, were engaged. President Mendenhall, along with many other communicants of the faith of the High Potential of women, has pointed out that life expectancy being what it is these days—especially for longer-living women—we must revise our timetables. It is absurd, in other words, for young women to rush into marriage. They obviously can have it both ways—career, at least a fling at it, *and* marriage. The alumnae magazine even published a cautionary article by Margaret Mead, "Dangers of Marriage in College," in which she pointed out that the college years should be an uncommitted time, a "moratorium" in which students can "explore, test, meditate, discuss, passionately espouse, and passionately repudiate, ideas about the past and future." She concludes by asking solemnly, "May it not be a new barbarism to force them to marry so soon?"

This kind of propaganda has made itself felt. The girls may still have their eyes on early marriage, but they are less smug about it than they used to be. A nineteen-year-old girl, engaged to a twenty-year-old stripling, said almost deprecatingly, "We're very young, I know . . ." And there has been some reaction against mandatory pairing off. One girl spoke approvingly of St. Anthony's at Yale where "it's not twosie."

"Smith to bed Holyoke to wed" is the way a scurrilous couplet goes, handed down, with adolescent bravado, by one generation of Amherst boys after another. An erotic fantasy rather than a reality, it does reflect the image of Holyoke girls as somehow softer. The more familiar reality is the sight of couples embracing at 1 A.M. (check-in time) at the entrances of the houses, utterly unmindful of each other and of the Kingsmen, the local security guards, who have seen it all and look on with ennui.

I visited Smith shortly before the big Christmas dances. Some girls were disturbed at the false impression I might derive. "It's so middle class," one said disdainfully and expressed the wish that I would come at a more austere season—"when we're studying or at colloquiums."

The Christmas parties showed striking variations. Those on campus had no drinking, and some had a dispirited air. In one house, a group of young collegians, impeccably garbed in evening clothes, played bridge in the lobby, while in the ballroom—a converted dining room—the orchestra was playing its brains out. At the hotels in town, however, students were drinking and dancing with considerable vivacity. But whether on campus or off the dancing, vigorous but inept, reflected the reduced estate of dancing among college students. As knowing as Smith girls are about most things, the pelvic vibrato of the cha-cha-cha has not yet infiltrated the Connecticut River Valley. (Many youngsters did a shambling fox-trot to Latin-American music.) "Dancing is a lost art," one professor remarked dolefully. And critic Elizabeth Drew said with merry malice, "They just put their heads together, creep around, and cuddle on the dance floor."

Some visitors watched the tame monogamy of the Smith students and their dates with a sense of mild outrage, recalling the more adventurous college dances of their time. Nowadays there are no stags, and each couple sticks doggedly together in a pale simulacrum of married life. President Mendenhall tried importing some stags for a sophomore dance. The reluctant draftees, feeling that they were somehow betraying their generation, refused to cut in.

But one social tradition has not changed over the years. Rahar's is still the magnet for students in time-honored fashion. Raffish, more beer garden than cocktail lounge, Rahar's is a student compound virtually off-limits to ancients over twenty-five. It is here that the encrusted gentility of Smith is put to rout, as boys and girls hunch over scarred tables thigh to thigh. Students out on dates converge here ritualistically. And the steaming, reeking, clangorous atmosphere acts as a kind of purgation. The small defeats in the classroom, the exacerbations of family, the ever-mounting pile-up of work, the stuttering terrors of sex—all of these are washed away, cleansed, in the ceaseless amber flow of beer.

An alumna staggered out of Rahar's after a visit insisting, "I haven't been to Rahar's since 1934, and I swear the same cigarette smoke is still there. I don't think they've opened the windows in all that time."

As in other privileged purlieus, class is an ever-present but never-mentioned reality. An alumna recently recalled, "The girls would turn up their coat collars and say they have to run to New York. The next thing we knew there was an announcement of their coming-out party in *The New York Times*."

"Who are the debutantes?" I asked a girl.

"You don't dare say," she answered.

In quest of debutantes, I visited a house—a shabby building soon to be condemned—reputed to harbor them. When I made known the purpose of my visit, there was a disgruntled silence. However, I became involved in a literary discussion—Karl Shapiro had just launched an attack on the sovereign power of T. S. Eliot—and when it became known that I am an academician, the attitude towards me became friendlier. Finally, one girl identified herself as a debutante. She was sitting on the floor in dirty chinos, wearing a sweater with holes at the elbows, her hair uncombed. She had recently had her coming-out party. "It was fun," she said matter-of-factly. Then she added with a shrug of her shoulders, "It was just a party."

Another girl in the house, a banker's daughter, revealed that her father's forebearance is stretched to the breaking point by just one thing. "Why," he grumbles, "must you wear *torn* sneakers?"

Junior year in Europe provides opportunities for that marvelous stretch of experience and vision that can occur only in youth. At the least, it provides release from the constrictions of class and from the green and pleasant prison house of Northampton. About one-fifth of the class goes, and for many life at home is never the same after the heady pleasures of the Continent.

There are programs set up for Italy, France, Spain, and Germany. The courses the girls take are carefully coordinated with their at-home curricula. But in Paris, the Seine and Montmartre are part of their campus; in Florence they move in an incredibly rich ambiance of art; and wherever they are, they live with European families. And they do all the fabled things: trips to the chateau country, mountain climbing in Switzerland, swimming on the Riviera. New England never looked so bleak and gray as when they return.

Since efficiency in the language of the host country is essential, most of the girls solemnly pledge to abstain from their mother tongue during their sojourn abroad. And a majority of them develop mastery of a foreign language—an achievement denied most

American students. (One girl complained that her immersion in French was so complete that her command of English declined— "I lost the big words!")

In an almost Jamesian way, the girls take on the coloring of the Old World. Some come back, in the tart phrase of one unregenerate stay-at-home, "pseudo-European—the kind that says, You people in America don't know how to live." And one girl announced grandly, "I can say with pride that in my junior year in Spain I didn't go out with a *single* American boy."

"I still haven't gone to a fraternity party," another returnee proclaimed, "and I can wait. A European boy is so much more mature. You come back here, and all the boys want to talk about is college weekends and how much they drank."

But the Smith girls also demonstrate that despite culture shock and high international drama, they remain staunchly themselves. "I never walked so tall or so straight," a girl said. "I would go into the Métro, put on my glasses and read a book, looking as staid as I could."

Nor does their sense of the absurd fail them when they confront some of the baroque features of European social life. One girl was courted by the son of the Spanish Pretender; she was only moderately impressed. Another girl in Italy lived with a high-toned aristocratic family who had a mad son. Others talked with amusement of the "Smith boys" in Italy, overage gallants who make a career of sorts romancing successive generations of Smith girls. "You think you've won someone's heart," a stunning girl remarked, "and then you discover he has been going with dozens of Smith girls. One girl has a Manfredo, and she still doesn't know if that's her predecessor's Manfredo."

Another girl added: "You think you're bringing America to some Italian family. Then they bring out the album, and they scream and sigh over the Smith girls of 1949–1950, 1950–1951, and so on."

An early Smith College catalogue described one of the school's prime subject areas as "lighter gymnastics in the open air . . . designed not merely to secure health but also a graceful carriage and well-formed bodies." Despite the air of well-bred introspection of so many of the girls, there is as much muscle on this campus as in any girl's college. The absence of men on campus propels girls into sports which in coed schools might seem downright grotesque. The girls play lacrosse, but as one bruiser put it, "You don't beat the other girl on the head." Smith is one of three schools with a crew but no football team. (Wellesley and MIT are the other two.) The mystique of the heavy oar and light shell was given a boost by the arrival on campus of President Mendenhall, an avid oarsman still for all his fifty years. It is his resolve, when pressures ease, to coach the girl's crew.

To be sure, there is something irresistibly Smithian about crew activity. The course narrowly skirts a waterfall, and there is always an apocalyptic vision haunting the girls of the shell tumbling over the brink, like some grim parable of the Fall. Indeed, on one occasion, two shells collided, and the girls in bulky parkas had to be fished out of Paradise Pond.

Students may take riding as part of their gym work, and about thirty girls stable their own horses on campus. They have a mock hunt course, but, gentle of spirit, they don't pursue any foxes.

Physical education has generated its own sniggering back-fence folklore. The girls are photographed once a year in the nude. The resulting "posture pictures" are used to improve body mechanics during the student's four-year stay. Recurrently, there are rumors —absolutely groundless, to be sure—of buccaneering Amherst students breaking into the vaults in the dead of night and stealing away with photos of nubile Smith maidens.

Smith's faculty is a teaching faculty. Teaching is central, and full professors often teach freshman courses. On the other hand, a three-day, nine-hour teaching schedule makes research possible. That, coupled with excellent students and country living, enables the school to maintain a superb staff. Another virtue of the Smith faculty is that a balance is maintained between men and women, unlike other women's schools which begin to look like secular convents. Smith professors include such distinguished figures as Daniel Aaron and Elizabeth Drew in English; Ruth Lee Kennedy in Spanish; Max Salvadori and Arthur Mann in history; and Gwendolen M. Carter in government.

Salaries are fairly good. The average for the entire faculty is $7,720, with instructors averaging $5,350 and full professors, $10,210. (Harvard's average for full professor is $16,000.) Since 1949–1950, salaries have virtually doubled, but they still lag behind the top colleges and universities.

There is a young-old split, with the young complaining that the Old Guard frowns on the lively, daring, and provocative. (A youngish artist on campus said sourly, "For the art historian, art becomes alive when it is dead.") The older professors hesitate to make a large personal investment in the younger members of the faculty since in these days of savage faculty raiding they don't know if the young professors will stay.

A woman instructor turned up with green eyeshadow, mascara, and a flamboyant mouth. An older woman on the faculty said quietly, "I guess no one has told her this is a conservative institution." The young woman soon changed into a good, gray faculty lady.

Life for faculty wives is difficult here, as it is everywhere. They bear the responsibility for maintaining a decent way of life on a salary often at the edge of penury. Nor do they have the satisfactions or the sources of renewal vouchsafed their husbands. There are always a few petulant wives—intellectuals *manquées* who feel that their towering minds are not sufficiently recognized. However, there are some distinctive virtues at Smith from the point of view of faculty wives. The school is not so small and intimate that they are kept busy baking cookies and doing other elegant trivia; nor is rank a source of dissatisfaction. One woman observed, "There's none of that dreary sense of hierarchy, with the wife of an assistant professor bowing and scraping to the wife of an associate professor."

A unique feature at Smith is the faculty-help program, in which students volunteer to serve as academic handmaidens to their professors. They lug books to the library, help with footnotes, or proofread manuscripts. As a reward, they are frequently cited in prefaces of books published by Smith professors.

Smith is a friendly place. Professors are often invited to have dinner at the houses. One professor made a plea for benches on campus: "The way things are now, you meet students coming out of the library or on a campus path, and although you both want to talk, you find it uncomfortable standing and shifting from one leg to another."

There is a calm expectation that the glory days of Smith during the administration of William Allan Neilson (1917–1939) will be revived by the current president, Thomas Corwin Mendenhall. Dr. Mendenhall is a tall, bald, invincibly good-natured man of fifty, who wears enormous horn-rimmed glasses and is helplessly addicted to bold checks in sport coats and to vaudeville capers. He was inaugurated in the fall of 1959 in a tide of good will, and since then, in the words of one observer, "has gone everywhere, met everyone, and charmed practically everybody."

An able historian, and a man of incisive mind, Mendenhall wears his learning lightly, has a robust sense of humor, and has already built up a reputable body of legend. His home on campus has inevitably been tagged "Uncle Tom's Cabin"; he is up absurdly early each morning for a quick turn around Paradise Pond in a one-man scull; and he is absolutely tireless about popping up at houses and having groups of students in for lunch-cum-discussion. The girls adore him.

The son of a Smith alumna, Mendenhall is fiercely evangelical about the value of a residential college for women. He quotes a high school senior who ingenuously remarked, "First you have to decide whether you want to go to a coeducational school or an educational one." In his inaugural address, he cautioned students against an unseemly preoccupation with marriage: "While any of us would welcome a happy marriage as a by-product of college education, to make it a first purpose is as wasteful of the precious resources of a college as it is dangerous." He sees the function of Smith as that of making sure "that both the student of chemistry and the student of classics catch the same vision of greatness and share for the rest of their days that common response to quality which is true culture."

The father of three girls, Mendenhall is as inundated by a female tide at home as he is on campus. His daughters were sulky about leaving Yale, where he was an associate professor, with its as yet untapped resources of young men. "All I can say," said his youngest testily, "is that I hope they're making it worth your while."

Smith girls are constantly berated by their faculty for their political torpor. "A timid skepticism" is the way one professor labeled their political posture. "Are the girls afraid to become *engagées* because they are afraid they won't become engaged?" asked another. "Convictions on tiptoe," snorted a third professor.

The girls engage in remorseless self-castigation. An editorial in *The Sophian*, while breathing a sigh of relief at the arrival of spring vacation ("escape from writtens, liberation from classes") exhorted: "As we go south for sun, let us keep our eyes and ears open, our senses awake, our concern alive to the less happy members of the student communities of America. . . . It doesn't take very much: a postcard sent to the national manager of the chain stores that practice segregation; a postcard sent to some of the students spending their spring vacation in jail or in court."

An earnest young lady, after hearing Norman Thomas talk about sane nuclear policy, wrote the school newspaper in perplexity: "What the heck am I going to do about it? Go to a cocktail party and smile benignly at the red cherry in the bottom of my whisky sour while advocating disarmament in a mildly feminine fashion?"

In truth, by current standards, Smith girls are vigorous activists. They pulled a boycott, dignified but airtight, on a local store that was overcharging; they picketed a local hotel after carefully investigating both sides in a labor dispute; and they lent support through picket line and telegram to Negro students engaged in lunch counter sit-in demonstrations.

The silver cord binding alumnae to their spiritual home is strong. There are 118 Smith Clubs blanketing the country and some European capitals. A recent issue of the *Alumnae Quarterly* rhapsodized about loyal Smith ladies: "They are wizards and wonder-workers, prophets and publicists. Literally nothing balks or disheartens a genuine Smith alumna . . . A gymnasium or a Students Building is assured almost as soon as its necessity is clearly seen. One stalwart in Westchester sold 8,544 pounds of pecans in the 1959 drive and contributed $5,500."

As many as two thousand alumnae turn up at Commencement and march with their respective classes, often bearing signs with announcements made by their professors decades ago. "The Alumnae Parade," one young woman said shudderingly, "looks like a pageant of the Ages of Woman."

All Smith women, past and present, have a compelling sense of time's stately processional—from the freshman who said excitedly, "Do you realize I've just taken my *last first* midterm?" to the proud alumna evaluating her life in preparation for the twenty-fifth class reunion.

The *Alumnae Quarterly*, in pages of close-packed print, keeps the women informed about the destinies of old roommates. Smith alumnae are impressively productive, alert, and far-flung. They do everything from managing ranches in Arizona to trotting dutifully after State Department husbands in Cambodia. Here are some sample jottings: "Eleanor (Smith) Godfrey built a contemporary house. She is getting her Ph.D. thesis on English glassmaking ready for publication . . . Frances (Hardy) Freezer is busy as Den mother and studying organ and French conversation . . . Betsy Deane bought a house in S. Lincoln, Mass. and will be back full-time at photography . . ."

Two faces of Smith alumnae, the genteel and the tough-minded, are revealed in a recent exchange of letters in the *Alumnae Quarterly*. A member of the class of 1913 objected to the term "odoriferous" used in a piece about the Congo dancers at the Brussels Fair published in the *Quarterly*. "The allusion was totally unnecessary," she wrote. "It was unworthy of Smith and the U.S.A." The editor-in-chief of the publication (class of 1928) responded bluntly: "I'm sure the Congo dancers smelled, and I'm just as sure that they would be the last persons in the world to care. I think it is our fussy civilization . . . and the television commercials on B.O.—all, I agree, in questionable taste—that make us so touchy about actualities."

Where does Smith go from here? At a time of great dynamism in higher education, the college knows that to stand still is to lag behind. Accordingly, there is an ambitious fund-raising program with a goal of $23 million in order to raise faculty salaries, and even to lure talented people from other campuses. (Small schools as well as huge universities can play this game if they have the money.)

Educationally, there is continued ferment. The future will see more science on campus and greater emphasis on non-Western culture. There is agitation from students for seminars in the first two years. Admissions being as competitive as they are, students are better prepared when they enter than they used to be, and some girls do not find college enough of a step up from high school. "Freshmen come expecting to be stimulated," a professor observed, "and if you don't catch them then, you lose them."

There is considerable revaluation going on among the students themselves about which way *they* are headed. Their animus is directed especially against the clubwoman image. "I don't want to go to a well-rounded school, marry a well-rounded man, and have well-rounded children," a girl said. Another deplored the goal of "living graciously in nonintellectual bliss." Others are distressed by the split between the social and the intellectual whose unsavory fruit is "the committee woman with just enough learning to be objectionable." There is some feeling on campus that they ought to dig out from under the mountain of extracurricular busy-work and get down to the intellectual core of college.

Smith College is in that curious interregnum which characterizes good colleges everywhere. At the same time that education is getting better, its established goals are being called seriously into question. Smith, no doubt, will change, but it will change in its own measured way, to its own drumbeat.

But no matter what curricular tempests rage, Smith will remain forever herself as long as there are girls like the freshman, overheard saying earnestly to a companion, as they passed through the venerable Grecourt Gates, "I'm beginning to think—I think."

SARAH LAWRENCE: for the Bright, Bold, and Beautiful

Sarah Lawrence College is peculiarly susceptible to parody. To the casual onlooker, the principle of excess seems enshrined. Its girls are extravagantly pretty. Its philosophy of self-expression, unabashed but not unbridled, has long been a sitting duck for wise-guy novelists and social caricaturists. And one of its cruelest ironies is that it looks most like what it admires least: an ultraswank finishing school.

The college consists of twenty-five acres of suburban wilderness, an outpost of rugged boulder and undulant lawn amid the encroaching apartment houses of Westchester County. Located in Yonkers, with a Bronxville address, Sarah Lawrence is the former estate of its millionaire founder, and its unspoiled terrain, handsome appointments, and Tudor elegance give an air of ease to an exercise in higher education which is, in fact, quite vigorous.

The reality of Sarah Lawrence is far less gaudy than its encrusted legends. It is progressive but guardedly so. It can, in truth, be charged with accommodating itself to the prevailing climate of conservatism. Former President Harold Taylor talked about cultivating "the homely virtues"; and the college tries to provide a solid substratum of discipline before the students make their flights into the empyrean of self-expression. A cool look at the program yields some sobering reflections about experimentalism in American education. This college, which one assumed was on the far edge of the experimental frontier, proves to be not too unlike other institutions. What has happened is that progressive ideas have, in some measure, been assimilated into educational practices even in the most retrograde colleges. On the other hand, the great experimental binge is over, and Sarah Lawrence, along with other schools, has been consolidating its gains and even undercutting some of its bolder features. Thus, colleges have tended toward a common middle ground.

Sarah Lawrence now has a new president. Dr. Paul Langdon Ward was formerly chairman of the History Department at Carnegie Institute of Technology. Though he is sensitive to the personality of the college—he sees the Sarah Lawrence girl as being more concerned about *both* education and world affairs than students elsewhere—he has not been identified with progressive or experimental education.

Ironically, progressive ideas in education, which had their matrix in the university-spawned philosophies of William James, Dewey, Whitehead, and others, have been applied largely to lower schools. (In the process, they have gone through an unhappy dilution.) Colleges generally remained impervious to them. The principal reason is that colleges are conservative institutions. Professors have traditionally been authority figures, and the college classroom enjoys a peculiar inviolability. Progressive ideas require a recasting of the teacher's role, an impairment, too, of his honorific status. He has to enter into a dynamic, uncharted relationship with his students. He has to involve himself in the dust and turmoil of the student's world. Who would willingly surrender the smug pleasures of the old relationship for the treacherous uncertainties of the new? Subject matter is much safer and stabler than students.

Nevertheless, progressivism has been seeping upwards to its own sources in the intellectual highlands. (Almost nobody uses the term progressive, to be sure; it has become pejorative, and educators employ tricky euphemisms. Sarah Lawrence, to its credit, does not run away from the word.) Colleges now imitate junior high schools in providing integrated courses in social sciences or sciences, and the interdisciplinary movement is what lower schools call the core curriculum. Many colleges now have departments of personnel service, which are merely a carrying onward and upward of high school guidance. And what college does not talk about meeting the individual needs of its students?

Teachers College may be scorned in the haughty purlieus of old-line academia, but it is actually victorious—except that most academics don't know it. The triumph of progressivism is muted, discreet, and gradual.

Colleges, then, have been catching up with Sarah Lawrence, but the latter—along with Antioch, Bennington, Reed, and a few others—is still way ahead of the academic procession.

The Sarah Lawrence philosophy is orthodox Deweyism with a heavy overlay of an older bookish emphasis. The individual and her interests are the center of the educational process. The line of movement is from the student to the curriculum. In traditional colleges, the curriculum is unshakably there, and the assumption is that the student and the courses will somehow connect. (One way, hardly the best, of making them connect is the cash-nexus of the passing grade.) Sarah Lawrence hews to other progressive ideas. Learning is the *active* use of knowledge, and facts must issue in judgments. Education should be stanchly concerned with the contemporary world—its realities, ideas, and issues—and should reach back to the past not for its own sake, but to understand the present. It upholds liberal values at a time when power, according to Dr. Taylor, is being wielded by the illiberal. (Like Harvard, Sarah Lawrence responded to Senator McCarthy's bullying with disdain. A crusty trustee of the college, a Republican from way back, said simply, "Never mind him. Teach school!") It is concerned with the arts as part of the curriculum, and it tries to combine practical experience with academic study.

Sarah Lawrence approaches the individual student with an almost religious awe of her potentialities, yet it is also socially minded and energetically activist. It is at once aristocratic and democratic, practical in its bent and high-flying visionary. The wife of the founder—the college was named after her—can help explain some of these contradictions. She has been described as "an old-fashioned progressive woman." One should remember, too, that in 1927, when the college got under way, the emphasis was purely on the individual; the social orientation came later with dark urgencies of the Depression.

How are these ideas translated into a day-to-day program at Sarah Lawrence? As the center of the educational process, each student formulates her own program in accordance with her interests. The assumption is that her course of study will fall into an organic shape in accordance with her own individuality. In practice, this can lead to a lumpy compote determined by hazily defined interests and fugitive whims. Some students use the college as a kind of cultural smorgasbord.

There are, however, institutional controls. The program, according to Dr. Taylor, is not "an invitation to the vulgar display of the raw ego." The college is alert to the dangers of narcissism and insists that "students give something back." The student plans her program with her don or tutor. Moreover, there are exploratory courses in the main subject areas which are suspiciously like General Education courses elsewhere. In actual practice the four-year program shows increasing specialization for some students, for others a broadening of interests as they move out from their own area to other related fields. For still others, there is a balance between their own field and other intellectual disciplines, not unlike the Harvard pattern of concentration and distribution.

At dinner with a group of Sarah Lawrence students, I asked for an example of a patterned four-year program. "Girls!" one bright-eyed student demanded across the empty coffee cups. "Who has a cohesive program?" (At a time when youth is so drearily middle-aged, there is a touching youthfulness in the persistent gap between the theoretical and the actual at Sarah Lawrence.)

The Sarah Lawrence girl takes only three courses a semester and gets a fat five credits for each. Most courses meet only once a week for a two-hour session. The rationale is that the student must be given time to read, to concentrate on what interests her when it interests her and not to be shuttled from one course to another in the usual four-year rat race. Former Dean Esther Raushenbush summed it up: "In other colleges students say, 'Who has time to read?' The fact that here our students have time to read conditions an attitude towards knowledge that will hold throughout life." Students read heavily for courses and in addition are expected to read for their dons.

In a school which eschews grades and the coarse-grained competitiveness one finds elsewhere, a curious quantification sets in. "We become competitive about the sheer bulk of reading," a girl said. "I feel unhappy if my roommate is reading *War and Peace* for her don, while I'm only reading *Death in Venice*."

The absence of grades creates yet another problem. Status is amorphous. "The only thing that rates around here," a girl explained, "is intelligence. But we have no way of measuring or appraising it."

Classes are small, seminar-size by the standards of other colleges. Each student has a weekly conference with every one of her instructors. At least one-third of the twelve to fourteen hours to be devoted to each course weekly is spent on individual projects. One student, for example, was able to do two years work in Italian in one year through this conference arrangement. The swift and the determined can get a great deal done in this fashion; those who goof off must face the weekly embarrassment of the conference. "This program," a dean observed, "creates the will to participate in education, not just to be fed." The arrangement also defeats the impulse students often feel to beat the system since they are joined with their teachers in one camp.

The Sarah Lawrence girl is constantly in contact with faculty. She sits across the table from them in small classes; she meets privately with course teachers and with her don. After hours she may attend a faculty-student seminar or help chart the destinies of the college. During Christmas and Easter, she may go junketing to Canada or Puerto Rico with faculty members in tow. This is a loving embrace from which there is little escape. Even during the summer she presumably is occupied in a way which has some relevance to her education.

The faculty itself is a classless society; there are no ranks, no slippery ladder to climb. There is, therefore, little of that fatal dissipation of energy in political maneuvering, in useless scholarship, that accompanies the careerist game elsewhere. This, coupled with the glossy reputation of the students and the proximity to New York, enables the college to recruit intellectual heavyweights like Horace Gregory, Joseph Campbell, Marc Slonim, Helen Merrell Lynd, Rudolf Arnheim, and others. Nor are they short-changed in the Ph.D. department. What the college looks for, it would seem, is the unstuffy Ph.D. in whom the scholarly rituals have deadened neither imagination nor the passion to teach.

The determination of the college to flee banality is sometimes amusing. The term *major*, associated as it is with old-line colleges, is anathema. "What is your major?" I asked a student. She looked at me balefully. "All right," I said resignedly, "what is your *field of concentration?*" "History," she answered brightly. And in the jazzy lexicon of progressivism, there are no course assignments; there are only *contracts*.

How does this program of individual education work out? For many students it yields extraordinary results. Some girls drive themselves in a way that they would not elsewhere. As one girl explained, "There are no standards here, no grades. At first it threw me. Then I realized it was for myself. I was the standard." But since the student's self is usually in process of definition, this can lead to a kind of intellectual self-flagellation. Students make inordinate demands on themselves that a formal course, with its neatly laid-out assignments, would not. Students talk dolefully of the "February letdown" and of the agonies of self-appraisal in the junior year, when the student is asked to "define herself." Until that time she travels at will in the realm of gold.

For some the program opens the door to indolence. Or its student-centeredness can lead to a fatal dispersion of the girl's energies. The college's emphasis on big ideas, rather than little facts—coupled with the students' free-wheeling creativity—can result in considerable diffuseness. "I've always had so many interests," a girl said. "Now they've doubled, maybe tripled. I'm so confused."

I attended a seminar at which faculty members discussed the relation of the social sciences to values. I was dismayed during the discussion period by student questions. The girls seemed at once overpoweringly verbal yet inarticulate. Many of the questions were diffuse or too broad, sometimes downright incomprehensible. I talked with Dr. Taylor about this intellectual haziness. "One of the things we do," he explained, "is to create an interest in larger issues. The student will cover ground once she becomes involved in ideas. What you see in these large questions is the first launching of this enthusiastic quest of ideas." A member of the faculty agreed with me about the sloppy questions and went on to say: "An education which is strong on discussion tends towards general ideas. Unless there is preparation on and control by the teacher, discussion can become diffuse. In class, that control is usually exercised."

College officials are alert to these dangers, and there has been some retrenchment in progressive ideas. "Human frailty is the weakness of our program," a faculty member said. "We expect so much . . . Sometimes if one asks for less, he gets more." The talismanic word on campus is now discipline. "We think of the creative spirit as needing discipline," Dr. Taylor said. "Some of the girls get the notion that it's the purity of psyche that counts, but the college is also concerned with the homely virtues."

A faculty member remarked, "I'm not at all sure that the kids have developed a stockpile of knowledge to enable them to follow their own interests effectively." Because of this feeling, General Education has slipped in through the back door. "We see to it that our students get some basic education," a teacher said. Some teachers now give exams, something unheard of in the old days. On Graduate Record Examinations, Sarah Lawrence performs creditably except in mathematics and the sciences.

Cynthia Robinson, a talented off-Broadway actress, recently recalled her freshman year at Sarah Lawrence: "I found my notes on Plato with such remarks as 'good, true, remember,' and on Nietzsche, 'bad, wrong, God is not dead.' When I came here I began looking for answers to things. Perplexed by man's destiny, I asked Mr. Trinkaus whether other students thought as deeply as I. He replied he didn't believe I thought deeply at all—which was quite a blow to my ego. My first report in Exploratory Social Science stated that I would have to learn to be content with working on the preliminary questions of philosophy before attempting the grand questions of the universe . . ."

At a time when college catalogues, in their avant-garde ebullience, often sound as if they were written by an editor on loan from *Partisan Review*, Sarah Lawrence's course titles are staid and conservative. Its catalogue abounds in such close-to-the-vest offerings as American Political Institutions, Romanticism in the Nineteenth Century, and Introduction to Psychology. Only the presence on campus of some commuters from the New School insures some measure of intellectual swashbuckling. Thus Marc Slonim, a distinguished critic, offers a course in The Hero in Western Literature.

Sarah Lawrence College has been the victim of a runaway folklore, which, in the manner of such things, tends to be self-canceling. Thus, the Bronxville campus is depicted as ultrasnobbish yet low-down bohemian. (An applicant, upon seeing the gaping holes in students' dungarees, quickly steered to the safe harbor of Barnard.) To Philistines, its artistic preoccupations are suspect, while to traditionalists its free-style intellectualism raises doubts. Most of all, the combination of girlish enthusiasm, good looks, and self-expression with the throttle open has proved irresistible to satirists. To some people, the college is merely a place where rich girls indulge their expensive whims. And there is still some lingering suspicion about the college's advanced politics.

A story by J. D. Salinger committed the solecism of lumping Sarah Lawrence with Bennington in this fashion: "The Bennington–Sarah Lawrence type looked like she's spent the whole train ride in the john, sculpting or painting or something, or as though she had a leotard on under her dress."

There seems to be an almost wilful tendency to misinterpret the college. A few years ago some Dartmouth students visited in order to do an article for their college newspaper. While sitting in a student dorm, the phone rang. The visitor lifted the phone and heard at the other end, "This is Harold Taylor." This was gleefully reported as "This is Harold," and a legend was spawned about first-name comradeship at Sarah Lawrence.

The college suffered a double wound in recent years when Mary McCarthy and Randall Jarrell went on a satiric jag in novels presumably about Sarah Lawrence. Some faculty people were convinced that Miss McCarthy was really writing about Bard College, another progressive institution in which she had also deployed her talents. Mr. Jarrell was dismissed as a "foot-faulter" in tennis by one irate instructor. The students appear to have read neither novel. "We're too busy reading really good books," a girl said with frank malice.

I discovered that the students stoutly resisted any discussion of a Sarah Lawrence type. If there is any shibboleth students are attached to these days it is that there is no homogeneity among them. In a conformist age, uneasy about its conformism, the great heresy is to admit it. Though there is no single image of Sarah Lawrence students, there are some generic tendencies.

The girls are likely to come from relatively sophisticated homes, and in time they will fill the ranks of upper bohemians. Their fathers are usually professionals or "enlightened" businessmen. The girls may be caparisoned in leotards, in a chemise, or more usually in sensible college girl clothes ("There are no unwritten laws about dress here"). In warm weather they prowl their campus barefoot in Bermuda shorts. Their hair is often long and unfettered. They tend to be good-looking—sometimes with a somber, brooding quality, more often in that fresh-faced, blatantly wholesome way that is the special delight of the celebrants of the American way of life. Occasionally one sees a stunning theatrical type who looks like a showgirl implausibly studying anthropology (she is likely to be a theater or dance major). The number of girls matriculated in four-times-a-week psychoanalysis is probably a little higher than at other campuses. It was reported to me by three alumnae that only girls in analysis were permitted to maintain cars on campus, to enable them to make their psychoanalytic sessions on time.

A visiting Williams College student characterized the Sarah Lawrence girl as a "cross between Bennington and Smith." The description makes sense. Somewhat more chastened in their view of the glories of self-expression than Bennington girls, the Bronxville students are less hidebound by academic tradition than their contemporaries at Smith. New York, only a half-hour away, is an escape hatch and saves the students from that febrile ingrownness that reportedly infects Bennington way out there in the Vermont hills. A transfer student from Smith made a pointed distinction, "Smith is *academically* stimulating, but Sarah Lawrence is *intellectually* more exciting." Another transfer student wrote in the school newspaper: "One difference between Sweet Briar and Sarah Lawrence is that Sweet Briar girls pride themselves on being intelligent but not appearing so, and Sarah Lawrence girls on both being and appearing intelligent."

"My friends are strung out in a variety of interest groups," a girl said. The school newspaper reports the activities of a bird-watching group and a cha-cha-cha class with equal enthusiasm.

Sarah Lawrence girls are irrevocably middle class, but they play at the cult of the peasant. "We go in for greasy hair and leotards," a girl said, "and the next minute we're shiny-faced. I guess we're a little of both."

This duality is reflected in their reading habits. According to the library staff, both D. H. Lawrence, the miner's son with his stress on the dark tides of emotion, and Henry James, the expatriate patrician, are the most popular novelists.

"I enjoy walking around Greenwich Village in heavy black stockings," a girl observed. "We play at Bohemianism here but not in earnest. It has no shock value."

The artistic-bohemian afflatus has undergone a stringent modulation in recent years. The single largest occupational goal is teaching, which attracts 18 per cent of the students. Almost one-third of the graduates go on to graduate work. This represents a considerable increase over the last few years, although the figure is a little lower than that of old-line women's colleges like Bryn Mawr or Barnard.

Social life at Sarah Lawrence is different from college norms. The sense of privacy that a woman's college affords means less pressure about dating. Social life does not confer prestige. Nobody asks, "How many dates did you have this week?" The girl who enters the dining room dressed for New York will elicit not "Lucky you!" but rather "How can you take the time off?"

Sarah Lawrence has a fair share of Social Register girls. A debutante, dressed in rough tweeds, her face innocent of make-up, told me that there is no real conflict between her college life and her outside social life. She goes to coming-out parties, she declared with sturdy common sense, "only to meet boys." However, Sarah Lawrence has stepped up her standards, and she finds most of the members of the social elect "unstimulating." Other girls express the same problem. "I find that I can out-articulate my dates," a literature major said.

The college has not yet worked out an entirely satisfactory social pattern. The proud intellectualism of the girls forbids their being too enterprising about dates. And though the college is near New York, as a West Virginia girl observed, "All right, so you get out at Grand Central. Then where are you?"

The urge to marry is not quite so importunate at Sarah Lawrence as it is elsewhere. About 10 per cent of the graduating seniors are married, with another 10 per cent on the brink. The quest for self-realization probably delays marriage. One girl said, "Marriage is difficult because here you're encouraged to think about yourself. How can you give to another person after Sarah Lawrence?" The college, by maintaining strict requirements for on-campus attendance, tends to discourage early marriage. President Taylor has decried the tendency to rush into marriage as an "escape from hard choices." Inevitably, he points out, it pulls talented girls out of college.

An instructor, discussing *Man and Superman*, remarked to his class, "Your generation's involvement with home and family is a good thing." A girl shot back impulsively, "How awful!"

Classes at Sarah Lawrence are small and fiercely intimate, the lines of communication between teacher and students tautly drawn. The atmosphere tends to be intense, hushed, almost reverential. I was struck by the fact that active participation was limited to just a handful of girls. There was never total disengagement—that would be rude. At the very least, students maintained a kind of sleepy vigilance. Yet some students have testified to the pressure they are under to contribute to class discussion. One girl declared, "At Sarah Lawrence I talked in class for the first time since high school." The truth is that the network of relationships is so sensitive that a Sarah Lawrence teacher would hesitate to wrench a girl out of the nest of her withdrawal, though he might raise the issue in his weekly conference with the student.

In the classes I attended, the intellectual energy level was a little low. Missing was a slambang exchange of ideas by which students can test themselves against their teachers. It is true that girls are more submissive than men students, but most teachers can recall women students who asserted their ideas with ferocity. The difficulty at Sarah Lawrence lies in the very effectiveness with which faculty-student closeness is built. They are joined in a common enterprise, and there can be no breaching of their unity. They reflect a *we-ness* that contrasts dramatically with the sense of *otherness* that students have elsewhere. At Sarah Lawrence, for example, a science instructor regularly brings coffee and doughnuts to class for his handful of students. At Brooklyn College, on the other hand, I have heard students in the hall refer to their instructors with the grimly impersonal *he*.

A member of the Sarah Lawrence staff who taught at Brooklyn College during the stormy days of student intransigence stated: "At Sarah Lawrence, the students are not intellectually aggressive. They don't try to pin the teacher down; they will back down in an issue. You see, they are enormously sensitive to the implications of any conflict. Arriving at a reasonable compromise seems more important than winning a point. The prevailing intellectual climate influences this. There's a recognition that problems are complex and perhaps not soluble in any final way. It may be, too, that our students have no real commitment to ideas. They may traffic in ideas, but that's quite another matter. On the other hand, when I taught at Brooklyn College, students learned through conflict who they really were."

It may be, too, that small classes, despite their undoubted advantages, lack the bounce and vitality of larger ones. This has been my experience as a college teacher. Interestingly enough, an alumna told me that the one lecture class she had attended at Sarah Lawrence was immensely successful. The instructor was Joseph Campbell, a man of powerful mind and persuasive charm.

Sarah Lawrence students face the usual dilemma of maintaining their femininity without sacrificing intellectual vigor. Some meet the problem by adopting the posture of earnest but not combative citizens of the Republic of Letters. (A college president told me that in his teaching days he gave up a job at a women's college because it was fundamentally corrupting; one can attain much too cheaply a sense of one's omniscience.)

Ironically, in a college evangelical about the individualistic ethos, there is a certain Organization character. Sarah Lawrence is a sensitive, other-directed community—a kind of loving despotism—whose members are too responsive to each other's needs to assert their own too boldly. Also, the college community in many ways is faculty-dominated. Students are consulted at every turn, they chair the meetings, and they make large pronouncements;

but the very respect for large ideas that the college inculcates insures that the teachers will predominate. Nor is this necessarily a bad thing. It is one way of keeping too much permissiveness in check.

Faculty-student intimacy is reined in by a pervasive sense of decorum. The donning system, in which a faculty member acts as a mixture of academic Nestor and personal counselor, can lead to an unwholesome probing for psychic ties. However, the don keeps hands off personal problems unless there is a clear and present danger to the student's intellectual efficiency.

The fact remains that Sarah Lawrence is fundamentally a good women's college with an unremitting sense of propriety—blood-sister to Wellesley, Radcliffe, and other citadels of upright young womanhood. High school seniors know this, and more than 900 of them apply for the 125 openings in the freshman class.

The college turns out a large corps of teachers. (One uncritically expects off-beat career choices from this realm of leotards, introspection, and resident composers.) Sarah Lawrence graduates make good teachers because they have been taught by good teachers, and good teaching is the heart of the program. The college's teacher-training pattern offers a bracing object lesson to the educational world. At a time when some prospective teachers are bedeviled by flaccid pedagogy courses, Sarah Lawrence prepares teachers and obtains the necessary accreditation without any sacrifice of intellectual nutriment. The system is amazingly simple. The college just doesn't have any education courses. Appropriate training is provided on an individual basis through cognate courses. Thus, the apprentice teacher studies educational psychology in her psychology class, principles of education in philosophy, and the history of education in European history. To be sure, this arrangement is made possible by small conferences and weekly conferences.

The creative arts, with a leaning towards the untried, the experimental, and sometimes the giddy, have been part of the Sarah Lawrence landscape from the start. Modern dancer Jean Erdman recalls having been catapulted into dance when Martha Graham was teaching there. Dr. Taylor's speeches probably had a higher literary quotient than those of any college president; he used to quote casually from Dylan Thomas, W. H. Auden, and Christopher Fry; Martha Graham is as likely to pop up in one of his talks as Bertrand Russell.

But even in the arts, there has been some recession from earlier fervors. The performing arts people are looking for balance. Until her senior year, a performing arts major may devote only one-third of her time to her field. And even in her senior year she will evoke disapproval if she is guilty of too much artistic parochialism. "You don't come here to be a studio fixture from 9 A.M. to 8 P.M.," a pony-tailed dancer said. "They won't let you." On the other hand, though the interconnectedness of things is stressed, students are no longer as busy cross-fertilizing the arts with the intellectual disciplines as they used to be. They steer clear of expropriating big cosmic ideas as subject matter for dance. "I don't find Occam's *Razor* or St. Thomas Aquinas serviceable in dance," a dancer announced primly. Suspicious of verbal athletes, dancers are prone to say, "If you can say it in any other way, you're not a dancer."

But the heartening thing is that Sarah Lawrence has not repudiated its brave, venturesome beginnings. It still hovers protectively over pale experimental efforts. A few years ago the college presented a new theater piece, *The Zodiac of Memphis Street*, a poetic play for dancers, actors, and musicians. In an idiom of stubborn inscrutability, the work was described as experimenting "with the time scale of the various performing arts . . . the dance and music convey what is happening on the emotional level, adding new dimensions, commenting on the action, adding meaning, and in the playwright's words, 'opening the moment.' " The moment was opened before an audience as chic and intellectually hep as one is likely to find in the New York area—svelte Bronxville matrons and their executive husbands, and a delegation from New York's artistic fraternity. (The community takes a proprietary interest in the college, but a taxi-driver said churlishly, "The girls should be learning how to cook.")

The college is equally ambitious in the realm of ideas. In a burst of Faustian energy, a two-day conference on contemporary American literature considered sweeping problems that in a less headstrong institution would be deliberated for a year. The conference swiveled from the relationship of literature to sociology, psychology, and religion to look at the tragic hero, humor and satire, and new movements in poetry.

A vital part of the Sarah Lawrence program is the integration of academic work with firsthand experience. This may take the form of assisting in a nursery, doing a survey of community attitudes, or a full-panoplied field trip during Easter or Christmas vacation. The field work is designed to back up the intellectual activities of the students. "We try to jolt our students out of what they're doing by new experiences," Ed Solomon, the director of field work, explained. "They get images of what they're reading and discussing, and then the experiences are fed back to the courses."

Thus, T. S. Eliot's jeremiad against industrialism was vivified for visiting students in small Quebec villages where they perceived the striking cleavages which have developed between the older and younger generations.

For Sarah Lawrence girls, insulated as they are by class and family, field work sometimes provides what Mr. Solomon describes as "culture shock." A group of girls returned from Puerto Rico one Easter with an acute sense of the limitations inherent in being urban and upper middle-class. Even more striking, in a period of sluggish social sensitivities, was the social passion that the experience excited. The girls had been quartered in small villages, where they trailed after rural leaders engaged in liberating the country folk from ignorance, disease, and poverty. It was a stirring experience. In the fashion of the thirties, they felt the pull of simple people and a deep urgency about their problems. After tearful partings—most of the village leaders called them "Daughter"—they returned to San Juan and the University of Puerto Rico, where they were outraged at the chancellor's calm, impersonal assessment of the vibrant realities they had just seen. (Another instructor remarked that many of his students, surfeited with ease, envy his having grown up in the thirties, in a period of strikes and evictions.)

The mid-thirties at Sarah Lawrence offer an interesting counterpoint to the present. This was the Age of Politics there as elsewhere. The most popular departments were the social sciences and psychology. Girls going out on field work often elected to serve in factories, union offices, or New Deal agencies. During the Spanish Civil War the girls voted to have meatless Tuesdays as a fund-raising device for Loyalist Spain. The well-to-do girl who resisted the stern voice of social conscience was likely to be asked, "Who do you think you are to go on living in a dream world?" The culture heroine on campus was the daughter of an honest-to-goodness coal miner. (Nevertheless, most of the girls still dated Princeton and Yale boys.) An alumna recalls that she was introduced to modern dance at a political rally on campus where grim-visaged girls danced *The Silicosis Blues.* Another feature of those early days was the presence on campus of a host of young faculty members. There were so many faculty-student marriages that Miss Constance Warren, president at that time, looked askance at hiring any more single men.

Sarah Lawrence's newspaper is a far cry from Harvard's *Crimson.* The contrast is instructive. Amateurish where the latter is professional, ingenuous where the *Crimson* is cool and sly, Sarah Lawrence's *Campus,* in its young ardor, throws away journalistic objectivity to scold, admonish, or exhort its readers. In a routine account of a lecture on Darwinism, the reporter suddenly erupted: "I am surprised that more students don't take advantage of this lecture series. We have long claimed that our foul attendance at social get-togethers was justified by our boiling interest in educational affairs. If we have this sober dedication to scholastic ritual—then where are we at 1 o'clock on Tuesdays?"

Like any experimental program, the college has its small absurdities: the student who in a discussion of the New Criticism rejects an idea with the peremptory statement, "But I can't *feel* it!"; the casual baby-sitter, out to make cigarette money, solemnly taking notes about the experience; the faculty member whose scholarly specialty is cultural attitudes towards cleanliness ("With the provocative question, 'Is it really good to be clean, or is it better to be a little dirty?' she launched into her favorite subject"); the college gate which says merely: "Tennis courts reserved for faculty and students only." (A student tried in vain to have the sign removed or at least the name of the college added.) Unfortunately, unlike Harvard, the students have little capacity for a purgative humor. It may be because of the youth and special vulnerability of the college. It may be, too, that the strong sense of mission that both students and faculty have, neutralizes the talent for laughing at themselves.

But self-criticism is chronic and remorseless. At present there seems to be a ground swell of opposition to educational shapelessness. A senior said firmly, "I want to know Homer's dates." A girl who visited Radcliffe reported that she was "impressed with the attitude of studying for a good grade on finals." (But she was also "shocked at the professors who often lectured with the pomp and circumstance of a stage performance.")

A Sarah Lawrence graduate, now in the theater, reminisced about her college days. "I received the degree of B.A.D.—Bachelor of Arts in Dilettantism," she said sulkily. "And notice what the initials spell—b-a-d." Then, pondering a moment, she added, "No, the scheme of education wasn't really bad. It's that we weren't good enough for it. I could get a lot out of it now." She described herself as half-educated at best. I pointed out that most college graduates are only half-educated. "But I *know* I'm half-educated!" she snapped back. This would suggest at least one of Sarah Lawrence's virtues: it offers an ambitious concept of the educated person against which the student can measure herself.

At a recent commencement, a student, Julia Carroll Whedon, gave a talk which was a witty, bitter attack on the silly machinery of modern education. Though, in effect, she was criticizing Sarah Lawrence at its worst, the talk reflected the college at its best. Confronting a "breakdown in expectation" from young people, she explained it in terms of the "beat whole child," the hapless victim of too much understanding. "Our lives are one big family album," she said. "When we feed we're not hungry—we're oral. . . . The ability to love is perceived as participation in some monstrous mythological event: the Oedipal Dilemma." Unlike her Harvard contemporaries who make a virtue of detachment, Miss Whedon called for commitment as an obligation in order "to rise above the limp predictions and the lame expectations."

There is an authentic generosity of spirit among Sarah Lawrence students, and a flair for enthusiasm all too rare among college students in these fattening sixties. A member of the faculty announced to his students: "When you are twenty years old, you have visions and ideals which you will never have again. If you are sensitive, they will sustain you for the rest of your lives. If you are daring, you will try to reach them." Sarah Lawrence girls try earnestly to reach them. In the drab landscape of student uniformity and prudence, they provide a vivid slash of color. The college has that *peculiar potency* in shaping values that a recent study found sadly lacking in most schools. And it may be from such quarters that a resurgence of American student life may take shape.

THE UNIVERSITY OF MICHIGAN:
Graduate Limbo for Women

A D. H. Lawrence scholar at the University of Michigan mused about how that writer, so passionately absorbed in the role of woman, would react to women graduate students. "I think Lawrence would see a certain smallness and dispiritedness about them," he said. "Yet many of these women students are attracted to Lawrence. I think it's partly their desire to be genuine women since they [women graduate students] are outside the pale. In *The Rainbow*, Lawrence deals with a high school teacher and the exhaustion that comes from controlling kids. I guess he would feel the same about graduate students."

People talk this way about the woman graduate student. The stereotype is grim and forbidding. In her manless state, the legend goes, she prowls the alley-ways of academia out of sheer desperation. She is alleged to be formidably plain, a girl who does little to improve her natural disadvantages. Most cruel of all is the charge that she is aggressively intelligent, maimed by a fatal confusion about what should be her authentic feminine role.

"They're just out of it," a flip woman undergraduate said dismissively. "They don't have any pizazz; they're kind of unloved and unhappy. And eh, how they dress! Full cotton skirts and sturdy brown oxfords with ripple soles!"

Why is there such an incredible disparity between the official portrait of the American coed—all winsome bust and rump and lively chatter—and that of the woman graduate student whose crabbed lineaments are reminiscent of nothing so much as the Museum of Modern Art's haunting show of neurotica titled "New Images of Man?" The coed and the woman graduate stu-

177

dent are so little separated by time, why is it they are so far apart in spirit? Graduate study is becoming popular these days, and women, though laggards, are flocking to graduate schools all over the country. (The figures for 1957–1958 show that roughly 198,000 men and 80,000 women were enrolled as resident, degree-hunting graduate students—an all-time high.)

Why do women go to graduate school? What sort of lives do they lead there? Are they academic stalwarts, or, as some assert, displaced persons lost in dusty library stacks?

I took these questions with me on a visit to the graduate school at the University of Michigan—one of the great centers for advanced study in this country. Located in Ann Arbor, forty miles from Detroit, the University of Michigan dominates the town. It *is* the town. In fact, it has spilled out of the narrow confines of the community and has a new North Campus—largely devoted to scientific research—just outside of Ann Arbor. The statistics of the university are awesome. The land, buildings, and equipment are capitalized at over $205 million. The school comprises 19,946 acres of very expensive real estate, 141 major buildings, and accommodates 24,000 students. The campus is a crowded one, with buildings reflecting the hundred-year growth of the university. There are grimy old Victorian piles with the legend "Chemistry" or "Classics" over the entrance, quaint mementos of the days when a little building could house an entire department. And there are gleaming new structures, all glass and red brick, which have sprung up in profusion during the current educational push. The university is not distinguished for the beauty of its campus —it is far too congested for that. But it turns out an impressive product; in recent decades, *Who's Who in America* has listed more graduates of the University of Michigan than of any other college—and that includes Yale and Harvard.

The country over, graduate schools size each other up remorselessly; even obscure little undergraduate colleges are kept busy grading the giants. Although there is no official ranking of graduate schools, there is a kind of crystallized quasi-official gossip about which schools, and which departments are up and which are down. (Undergraduates, in fact, learn about where to go for graduate study from their professors whose eyes are cocked on the national scene. Each academic area or discipline has national, even international boundaries, and what happens at Berkeley or Harvard or Michigan is of intense interest everywhere.) According to a recent poll of heads of graduate departments in leading universities, the University of Michigan's Horace H. Rackham School of Graduate Studies ranks fifth nationally, surpassed only by the graduate schools at Harvard, California (Berkeley), Columbia, and Yale. Following Michigan, according to the poll, are such distinguished graduate schools as those at Chicago, Princeton, Wisconsin, Cornell, Illinois, Pennsylvania, Minnesota, Stanford, UCLA, Indiana, Johns Hopkins, Northwestern, Ohio State, NYU, and Washington, in that order. The unwary are reminded that these are approximate ratings and have no relevance to particular departments, which may be rated higher or lower than a school's over-all ranking would suggest. Michigan's graduate departments seem to hover around the level of the school's rating— a meritorious fifth. There are exceptions: Michigan runs second only to Harvard in psychology, third in philosophy, while its chemistry and economics departments rank fairly low among the academic behemoths.

The University of Michigan, in short, has a lead role in that efflorescence of higher education which is a feature of our time. It has its share of academic luminaries (anthropologist Leslie A. White, for example, well known for his cultural theory of evolution, and man of science George E. Uhlenbeck, codiscoverer of the "electron spin"). And it attracts first-rate graduate students. They come from all over the country, and from dozens of foreign lands as well, turning Ann Arbor into kind of a small, tree-shaded New York—impersonal, feverish, full of busy and preoccupied people. In a week at the university, only one student I passed said "Hello." There is little Midwestern bonhomie.

There are over five thousand graduate students at Michigan, of whom about 1,500 were women. There are, in addition, about 236 women among the roughly 2,700 students engaged in graduate-professional studies such as dentistry and medicine. During my visit, I made the rounds with women graduate students. I attended classes in which they are students (notebooks open, pens nervously busy), and where they teach (they merely switch from flats to heels). I surveyed their surprisingly decorous drinking places (beer only), looked in at their apartments (as neat and austere as monkish cells), and talked endlessly with them.

First, we should dismiss the nasty canard about their looks. If they are less than glamorous collectively, they are a cross-section of the young women of America, ranging from the breathtaking —a small minority—to the plain. What they have in common is an indifference to dress. Never were so many skirts and blouses slopped into service.

Why do they come? The stereotype of the unloved and lonely has only slender truth. At Michigan about 40 per cent of the women graduate students are married. Most elected to go on with their education for correct and wholesome motives. Single or married, they find that the B.A., except for elementary or secondary school teaching, is preparation all too often for only routine jobs. Professional requirements are scaled up these days, and increasingly graduate training, even the Ph.D., is essential for *interesting* work.

There are those for whom academic values have always been paramount. An anthropology student, with a blazing interest in American Indians, recalled, "My mother tells me that when I was born, I didn't let out a birth cry but a war whoop." Proudly this student showed me two photographs of herself—one as a pig-tailed five-year-old brandishing a toy tomahawk, and another as a graduate student, wearing authentic Indian costume acquired on a field trip.

Usually, the women who make it into graduate school were strong students all through college, and somewhere in their history there was a fructifying relationship with a professor, who helped them gradually to incorporate the values of academic life: the sheer pleasure of learning, the heady joys of discussion, the athletic exhilaration of tracking down a research problem.

There are those, of course, who merely drift into graduate work. "If a girl graduates from college and isn't engaged, what should she do?" a pretty girl asked. "She can go to New York for a career, but I like academic life, so this is what I did."

An M.A. candidate in mathematics, who had majored in education, said she simply didn't feel ready to teach. Her year at

Michigan was a buffer between college and the cloistered elementary school classroom—a kind of final sowing of academic wild oats.

Scholastic joys can be intense. Women graduate students at Michigan never worked harder, they say, never had a more grinding sense of how little they knew and of how much they have yet to learn. I watched a classics student hover with exquisite pleasure over a photograph of a Roman tombstone. She was attempting to restore the inscription—part of her work for a course in epigraphy. For another course, one in papyrology, she had just deciphered an original second-century papyrus from Egypt. (It turned out to be a prosaic receipt for wheat given to a landowner by a farmer as rent for his farm.)

Most graduate students find considerable nervous excitement in the search for, and discovery of the academic father, a distinguished professor who initiates the young person into the Sacred Mysteries of the Discipline. But at best, graduate study is a tough grind. Even professors comfortably ensconced in cushy academic posts rarely get sentimental about the grubby days of their apprenticeship. "The system beats you down," a male historian commented. Some graduate students tell you that academic life in a graduate school is less fun intellectually than undergraduate days. What they are complaining about more than anything else is the changeover from the role of cultural consumer—an agreeable role—to that of cultural producer. Not all Ph.D. candidates have an affinity for research (for instance, about half do none to speak of once the degree is safely in hand).

In graduate study there are massive, omnipresent pressures. First, there are the courses (thirty credits for the M.A., sixty for the Ph.D.) At the University of Michigan a grade under C does not count as graduate credit, and the required average is a robust B. Looming menacingly are foreign language exams and prelims, which are comprehensive exams frankly designed to liquidate the academically infirm. And after these fierce bouts there is the herculean struggle of the dissertation.

Each university has its own *modus operandi*. At some schools one merely registers for classes, attendance is optional, but Judgment Day overtakes the self-indulgent at the prelims or orals, and students pay then for every delicious Monday morning they slept late and missed class. Elsewhere, the courses are demanding, while the prelims and dissertation are almost a formality. At some places, students are looked after solicitously and shoved through the rat race by faculty sponsors; at others, they are desolately on their own—academic orphans, unloved and unwanted until they are close to the Ph.D. and show real promise. But graduate schools have one thing in common: one way or another, they are all rough.

Unlike the B.A., which is now almost as common as a driver's license, the Ph.D.—or even its poor, despised cousin, the Ed.D.—cannot be claimed as a democratic right. Candidates sweat and strain after the doctorate for five, ten, and even fifteen years—dazed inmates of a book-lined limbo—and the mortality rate is high. Almost any sophisticated cocktail party in a large city is likely these days to have a few aborted Ph.D.'s, many of whom, by the way, go on to distinguished nonacademic careers.

Often it is the dissertation that sends the scholars scuttling off into business. The squeeze is merciless. On the one hand, students are expected to work meticulously on their dissertations, to follow truth wherever it leads. On the other hand, they had better snap to it, for there is a rigid timetable for academic achievement. At Michigan, the doctorate must be attained within seven years, or there are penalties like taking courses and exams over—a demoralizing business!

After the massive effort of the dissertation, there is the wan ceremony of depositing three copies of the manuscript in the graduate school office. A 600-word abstract is prepared for *Dissertation Abstracts*. Then, in a symbolically revealing act, the dissertation is reduced to microfilm. And that is more or less the end of it, unless the brand-new Ph.D. starts to send it out to university presses for possible publication.

Graduate students lead a curiously straitened life, physically and intellectually. "You're isolated in little cells," a graduate student at Michigan said. "There are lots of buildings I've never been in and never shall. Occasionally, very occasionally, I'm aware that I'm on a college campus."

"You could die here," a girl said, "and the only way they would know is when the cadaver began to stink."

Another graduate student was acrimonious about graduate study as an *obstacle* to liberal education. "For people who just want to learn," she said, "I don't know if it's any good. You have to sort of sneak learning in between all those required books. There really ought to be institutions for intellectual people who don't plan to become professors." (A recent publication, *The Graduate School and the Decline of Liberal Education*, by Earl J. McGrath, makes much the same proposal; McGrath comes out boldly for reconstituting graduate schools as centers of liberal arts instead of specialized academic shops.)

The girls are prone to talk of their unheroic martyrdom with infinite relish. In an affluent society, they are a stubborn pocket of poverty, a slum in the nouveau riche suburb of academia. The financial take for professors in good universities is handsome, but for the female graduate student, life is skimpy. Chaucer's clerk of Oxford, with his lean horse and threadbare garb, has as his spiritual descendent the female academic. The men do nicely these days, thank you, between their grants and their spouses. (As a current gag has it, the graduate student lives by the sweat of his *Frau*.) But women keep alive the old tautology—the poor student. There are, to be sure, hundreds of teaching fellowships and grants; but men do better in this department than women, and even these rarely exceed $2,000 a year. The unmarried girls, therefore, are in a very low income group. Luxury items that enhance morale are usually excised—perfume, good cosmetics, decent clothes. The woman graduate student becomes that most sexless of creatures: an academic drone, indifferently dressed.

Worst of all, she often cannot make up her mind about the future. If she is merely an M.A. candidate, the internal pressures are comparatively mild. The end is in sight. But the Ph.D. seems like an interminable grind, a vast expense of spirit. *And then what?* The truth is that many women are academically motivated but professionally confused. Men rush headlong through the degree if they can muster the psychic and intellectual resources. But women tend to delay—and there is objective evidence of this.

A recent study at Harvard and Radcliffe, revealed that while 26 per cent of the men took from four to ten years to complete their Ph.D.—an excessive period—the percentage of dawdlers among Radcliffe women was even higher: 44 per cent. And the women delay for what seems to be a good reason. If they are single, getting the degree means an end to the interregnum between college and marriage. It means facing up to the next, even more terrifying, phase of their life. What next?

Next is likely to be a small, obscure college somewhere in the hinterland, for the juicy academic plums usually go to male Ph.D.'s. Ever more terrible, the next step may be that final entombment in a small *women's* college—no fate more harrowing than that. So the female graduate student bogs down in her dissertation. What's the rush?

As a result, the bitterness, the anxieties, the nervous fretting about is-it-worth-it are as real as the academic ardors. The girls love academic life, and they hate it. They hang on gamely in a giddy cycle of elation and depression.

"It's common to call up a friend here and say, 'What's new?'" a Michigan graduate student explains. "And someone will answer, 'Marian's cracking up today.'"

"We sometimes feel it's a kind of doom," a history student said dolefully, and then recited a bleak catalogue of the evils of graduate study: "Always having to prove yourself, not being able to read the novel you want to read, the tensions of prelims, being grown up and yet being told what to do, not being able to travel—you just get fed up with this sordid life."

Nor is there relief when they get home. A young woman from Milwaukee remarked, "You don't feel like an eccentric until you go home. In my city there's a fine German word they use for us—*überstudiert* (overstudied)."

A pretty Brooklyn College graduate reported that her classmates back in Flatbush describe her half-admiringly, half-scornfully as "idealistic." They add complacently, "We just went after that diamond ring and got it."

Small towns are even worse. A girl from a hamlet in backcountry Missouri runs the gauntlet of three questions every vacation: Are you still in school? When are you getting married? When are you coming back to Missouri to live?

Certainly, there is little in the social life of graduate school that would make an impressive tale to throw up to probing friends back home. On the face of things, graduate school is an unmarried girl's dream country—virtually a male harem. There are almost four men in the Michigan graduate school for every woman. But the resounding if extravagant lament about graduate men is: "They're either married—or impossible!"

The melancholy reality is that a girl can be a stunner and yet get lost socially: there are departments with a scarcity of marriageable men. The school of social work, for example, is heavy in women; classics has lots of priests. And there is little mobility. Unlike undergraduates who roam at will—meeting people of many kinds and in many fields through "activities" and their sororities and fraternities—graduate students do not often cross departmental lines. Girls date the men in the department. And the further they go in a field, the harder they find it to establish rapport with someone outside it. ("I'll have to marry in the profession," a philosophy student said. "Engineers bore me.")

Generally, there is little split between work and play. There is a good deal of relaxing during the day in departmental hangouts. Philosophy people, for example, foregather in the Commons Room, where they habitually have their lunch (a sandwich prepared at home, coffee from the hot plate). Other departments use snack-bars scattered through the buildings. (There are, of course, well-appointed dining rooms in the two student unions, but graduate students eat there only on state occasions.) At ten or eleven in the evening, after a long session of solitary labor, the hardier graduate students meet for a beer or a cup of coffee.

The social pattern is informal—sometimes bleakly so. (Nothing is so oppressive as mandatory informality.) There is no place to go—only student beer joints. Detroit is near enough but few graduate students have cars. And if they do (usually decrepit relics), it seems a senseless frivolity to go barreling around night clubs after a hard day of somber academic work. (One couple, appalled by the invincible squalor of their lives, got dressed one evening in all their finery and walked grandly to The Michigan, the local movie house.)

The evenings, in graduate school, are likely to be merely extensions of the days: academic discussion ("A cat is never a cat, it's always a symbol," an English major complained), gossip, love, if luck is there. Sometimes graduate students go to the Pretzel Bell, famed U. of Michigan drinking place, and wistfully look on at the standard ritual. (When a student reaches twenty-one, the legal beer-drinking age in Michigan, a huge bell peals in celebration, while the boy or girl stands triumphantly on a table downing schooner after schooner of beer handed up by jubilant friends.) But the graduate students are really out of it, estranged from these innocent pleasures as they are from the banks of the Huron River or the leafy bowers of Nichal's Arboretum, where, in the spring, undergraduates go to make love. That whole delightful if censurable side of American higher education in the college as playground for adolescents is firmly sealed off from graduate students. They live in an ambiance of undergraduate fun, but they may not reach out for it. Theirs is a new-found and chafing academic dignity.

"We're mostly friends," a girl said of the men in her life. "It sounds Jamesian, I know, but that's the way it is." However, relationships grow in depth, and, according to many girls, have "more substance than the fluffy undergraduate stuff." To be sure, dating the boy in the next seat has its asperities. "It's just too bad if he gets a B, and you get an A minus," a girl said. "But we don't want the weaklings anyway."

Another graduate student sketched a hideous portrait of the "hungry female": around thirty, with a Ph.D. or close to it, and no husband. She throws parties to which she invites young men in the hope they will come alone. (She hates and fears the pretty young things who turn up on these occasions.) The hapless hostess, according to this informant, almost invariably "ends up on the floor quite tight, snuggled up to one of these young men." Only slightly less disagreeable are the parties given by groups of such women relentlessly "trying to find someone"—a pursuit which effectively excludes fun.

Among the most abrasive features of this graduate-school life, women say, are the rebuffs they must endure from the masculine world. Given their own self-doubts, they find these assaults that come from smug masculine purlieus particularly punishing.

It may be disguised antifeminism, or it may issue from a realistic appraisal of their performance, but the conviction exists that women graduate students are not really in earnest and are less likely than ever to do distinguished work. "When it comes to night assignments on a research project," a psychology professor said peevishly, "they'll ditch me if they have a date."

Some professors feel cheated of the possibility of academic immortality when they have too many female students. The chance to transmit a body of ideas—canonization through disciples—is lessened by women, whose academic career is likely to be ephemeral.

A psychology professor, now an administrator, spoke of the antifeminist bias of his colleagues with startling candor: "I was struck by the geeing and hawing of the liberals in the department when they were faced with lots of good women applicants. The argument advanced was that we had limited resources and were faced with a dire need for teachers. And we had to consider the length of service candidates might offer. Some good women lost out as a result." He wishes society—and women—were more flexible. He would like to see part-time teaching jobs made available to married women, and some sort of retraining period arranged for female Ph.D.'s who absent themselves from the profession while their children are young.

One of Michigan's departmental chairmen thinks women ought to complete their Ph.D.'s not at twenty-eight but at forty-eight, when their child-raising chores are done, so that there would be no lag between their studies and their teaching. (Because she interrupts her career, the woman Ph.D. often teaches with a set of skills and a body of information ten or fifteen years out of date.)

Even praise of women graduate students is tinged with a certain condescension. "They have the right virtues," a dean observed. "They're neat and punctual." An English professor said: "They're more patient and systematic than men. They're likely to do very well with bibliographic problems [just about the dreariest area of literary scholarship]. Relatively few have shown marked originality. Very often they make good teachers of Freshman Composition because they're patient and diligent." (In most English departments, teaching Freshman Composition is viewed as a humiliating serfdom.)

These views, though not untypical, are nonsense. Given the right incitements, women could achieve as much in scholarship as men. They fail precisely in the measure they are made to fail. This is an example of what sociologists call "the self-fulfilling prophecy." Made woozy by propaganda, the girls in time see themselves as a minority group immured in a cheerless academic ghetto. (A shapely ex-model from Miami Beach, now implausibly installed as a teaching fellow in philosophy, tells with wry amusement that her dates ask her quite seriously, "Do you know how to dance?" The young men in that other, and now distant phase of her life, used to ask very different questions.)

A young woman, a Ph.D. in psychology, who often counsels graduate students sees them as a "special, self-selected group." She doubts that many girls go to graduate school merely because they have nothing better to do. "I wonder," she speculated aloud, "whether they would drop graduate work if they got married. They tend to idealize marriage. They overlook the tedium. If it comes down to it, I'm not sure they would give up their studies."

Certainly, there *are* many girls who have tried to make the best of both marriage and graduate study. For the most part, they manage very well. A political science major, whose sultry, theatrically sexy appearance belies a discerning mind, had a problem. She was getting married in June, and her fiancé—also a graduate student—was scheduled to go into the army. However, graduate work had just opened up for her in that first, exhilarating breakthrough when academic life begins to seem more like an adventure than a disease. She had received a grant for the next year, and was slated to some exciting research connected with the behavior of voters in the Presidential election. She finally decided to return to Michigan in the fall (instead of following her husband from army pillar to post), even though it meant forging ahead of him. Meanwhile, she has drafted the blueprint of their future career. Their academic areas overlap—she is in political science, while he is in sociology. "He's very creative and imaginative," she said, "but I am logical and systematic. He'll have the ideas, and I'll operationalize them."

A girl pushing steadily toward a Ph.D. in physics is married to a physicist with a mere B.A. "But he's brilliant," she expostulated. "Each of us has his own area of superiority." And physics dovetails neatly with the requirements of domestic life, for she is in the theoretical branch—"pencil and paper stuff."

Another young woman is studying art history; her husband is a Ph.D. candidate in anthropology. At exam time, there is a double strand of distress. "We beat the kids at the same time," she said. Money is tight, and so two nights a week she works as a waitress in a local espresso shop. "Sometimes at the end of a day," she mused, "I think of the things I've done and I'm entertained by the incongruities—looking after the kids, attending class, and then dressing as exotically as possible for the espresso place."

The life of the woman graduate student is full of such incongruities and ambivalences. "The further a young woman goes in the academic world," Michigan's dean of women observes, "the further she removes herself from the normal complex of wife and mother. This is the unseen drama."

But a few things are clear. Women are academically gifted, even if they are constantly being tripped up or tripping themselves up. As matters now stand, their resources are mostly going to waste—either rusting unused or dissipated in suburban boondoggling. And when they persist in using their skills, they are confronted with the unnerving question, "But don't you want to fulfill yourself as a woman?"

The problem will no doubt answer itself soon. The demand for college teachers during the next decade will be so intense that the barriers will topple. As more women join the ranks of graduate students, it will no longer seem a heresy when they devote themselves to the intellectual life. The gates of the ghetto will swing open.

AMERICAN COLLEGES:
A Summing Up

A friend of mine, a college dean and a mild insomniac, recalled that when studying for his Ph.D. in education at Harvard, he used a prominent journal of education as a soporific. Ten minutes of curriculum planning, and he was sound asleep. "It never failed," he said appreciatively.

That is one of the things wrong with education today—the stupefying boredom its high-toned idiom generates. There is hardly an educational journal written with grace and sophistication. But that is merely a symptom of higher education's ills. First, a grim statistic: the student drop-out rate is almost 60 per cent. For more than half its clients, the service that colleges render is unsatisfactory—or the customers ill-chosen. Second, we find failure when we look at the product—the college graduates. How many of them are shaped significantly by their experience? How many have developed the habit of disciplined thinking? How many, by decent standards, are well educated? Very few, the honest college teacher would acknowledge ruefully. It is just possible that professors and students are actors in a vast comedy, a mad travesty of solemn ritual, wasted time, and trumped-up claims.

During the last few years, I visited a dozen or more campuses, talked with presidents, deans, professors, and hundreds of students. I have also taught in college—both full-time and part-time—for a dozen years. What I offer here is the distillation of my observations. If they seem harsh, it is not that I lack tenderness for higher education. Americans have perhaps too much, born of the stubborn conviction that somehow education is a good thing. (Education is our secular church—the one faith that unites us all.) If I seem at moments critical, it is out of my conviction that education is too valuable to fool around with; we shouldn't permit it to settle into a bog of sloppy sentimentality and vested interests.

This is no dirge about the fall of valor. No doubt, colleges are better than they were a few decades ago. Students work harder; there is less nonsense. But the old mummeries no longer deceive. It is self-evident that higher education is not good enough.

We have imposed upon our colleges, as we have upon the lower schools, an almost hopeless array of tasks. Our educational goals are at once aristocratic and democratic, vocational and intellectual. We want our college students to be intellectual stalwarts, impassioned seekers after truth, but we insist also that they be regular guys and nice girls, skilled in ballroom dancing and badminton. We pull our curricula this way and that depending upon which ideology is in the ascendancy. And the students, caught in these cross-currents, are somewhat bemused.

They are nice enough kids—decent, good-natured, a little torpid perhaps. Their vision is pinched off by career and marriage and what passes for the good life on TV commercials. They want a degree—a visa for suburbia. What can we do with their four years of college to make of them more than trivial rites of passage?

In making the rounds, I was struck by the fact that schools divide into two kinds: those which we might call adolescent reservations, fenced off from serious adult concerns, and those which represent a transition to adulthood. Harvard is an example of the latter. If anything, there is at Harvard an expropriation of an unattained adulthood which can be disconcerting. The adult visitor is not only treated like a fellow-citizen of the republic of learning but sometimes like an apprentice. Nevertheless, I far preferred the condescension of Harvard striplings to the opacity I found elsewhere.

When I visited Harvard, I brought the inverted snobbery that only someone with a working-class background and a municipal college education could have. I came to scoff but remained to be impressed. No academic person could resist the exuberant play of ideas. It is a great university. Wisconsin offers a vivid epitome of American democracy—its strengths and weaknesses. Birmingham–Southern College provides a familial warmth that is preeminently Southern. Sarah Lawrence reflects a measure of intellectual daring that is still rare. Brooklyn College yields a solid education for a subway token. Claremont has a multicollege plan that may be tomorrow's answer.

One can hardly resist the fantasy of shuffling the elements of some of the schools. Birmingham–Southern could learn from some of Brooklyn College's intellectually bellicose kids, just as Brooklyn could profit from BSC's relaxed rhythms. Wisconsin's hurly-burly of farmer's son and storekeeper's daughter might dilute Harvard's tendency toward preciousness. There should be an infusion of Claremont's rugged optimism about higher education in boards of trustees all around the country.

What about size? There is no ideal size, but those huge city-states like Harvard or Berkeley or Chicago are naturally the ones we hear about most. It is important to remember that a university's reputation is usually based on its graduate schools, not on the quality of undergraduate instruction. Few people know this—except disgruntled undergraduates—for the great universities keep their reputations golden through research breakthroughs, Big Names, and books, books, books. What takes place in freshman composition or World Civilization I is of less moment.

The truth is that a small school is often better equipped to deal with the tenuous beginnings of intellectual life. A senior I met at the University of Wisconsin had transferred from a cornball college in Iowa. At the smaller school, she said, she wrote far more papers and had easier access to faculty. In fact, she assisted a political science professor as he journeyed about the district electioneering for a Democratic candidate. "I helped elect the first Democratic congressman in that district," she said proudly. At Wisconsin she became social chairman of the Student Union, but surely she must have had a wan sense of decline from the heroic days of routing out rural Democrats.

On the other hand, Dr. Conant's strictures against small rural high schools apply to colleges. There are small colleges tucked away in rural areas that are no more demanding than a good city or suburban high school. Our new educational egalitarianism—every citizen a B.A.—keeps them going.

"If you have a high school diploma and have stayed out of jail, then you can go to college," a critic observed tartly. The danger of this new stampede, according to Charles Frankel, is that "more and more Americans will be holders of degrees that mean less and less." The idea of college education for all is profoundly attractive. If only it worked! The high drop-out rate points up the limitations of the idea. And despite these scholastic casualties, standards have a way of accommodating themselves to the mass.

There is something to be learned from the municipal colleges of New York City. Here, free higher education is a birthright—but it can be exercised only by the able students. For the late bloomers and high school goof-offs and even for those who flunk out, there is a last-chance alley. The evening schools are designed as a kind of academic purgatory in which scholastic ne'er-do-well's can do penance, and the hitherto unqualified can demonstrate talents.

We live in an age of consolidation in education. There are few new ideas; most of those being argued about at the moment are simply old ones refurbished. Independent study is really the familiar tutorial, in which a student works on his own under the guidance of an instructor. Educational TV, despite its technical bravura, is essentially the lecture method. Actually, discussion about method often misses the point. More important than the specific method is the quality of the teacher. Even the so-called depth/breadth controversy is at bottom unimportant. Any significant attainment of depth—exploring limited subject matter intensively—will open broader areas of study. And a reaching out in breadth—survey courses are a good example—should provoke the student to explore some part in depth. Good teaching restlessly cuts across all methods.

But in the midst of the Great Debate, retrograde teaching plods on. Talk to students, and you can compile a bleak anthology of boredom, inertia, and ineptness among teachers. The unconscionable method of stuffing the "prolix gut" of the student—the phrase of Woodrow Wilson's—is still going on. "They just give you the text," a student said bitterly. Another remarked, "My professor throws something at us, and we return it on an exam. In between we never even look at it." Perhaps the most startling symbol of complacency and disengagement is provided by a very near-sighted professor I heard about, who removes his glasses so that he cannot see his students, sits back, and pontificates. Students are indignant at first about this dreary assembly line of learning. Freshman year, a time of the greatest expectations, is often a cruel disappointment to many who had looked forward to something exhilaratingly different from high school.

Right now the tides of controversy are swirling around the Ruml Plan, which envisions a flexible pattern of lecture, seminar, and independent study. Every student would experience all of these arrangements, in varying proportions, instead of the current mixture of lecture and recitation. It may well be that all discussion is academic, for, as one authority observed, "The Ruml Plan has to happen." The economies it offers provide the only feasible way of meeting the wave of students during the next decade. (It also presents a method of raising salaries, but even that has failed to endear it to faculties, a disputatious and chronically aggrieved group.) There is little doubt that the teacher-student ratio has been a sacred cow. The former president of Fisk University once observed that without a superior teacher, "the small class merely assures the transmission of mediocrity in an intimate environment." Available evidence suggests that the mere size of a class has little influence on educational efficiency. Even teaching machines, Orwellian as they seem, may have a legitimate place in rote learning. And the prospect of the best teachers in the country—even in the world—becoming available through TV and in kinescope is indeed persuasive. The academic profession would do well to give up its guerrilla warfare against change. (Academicians present the paradox of being liberals politically but die-hard conservatives professionally.)

Ironically, as matters now stand, American universities rely far too much on lecturing, without the other features that the Ruml Plan includes. The usual pattern provides large lecture classes, staffed by topnotch professors, with small sections covered by graduate assistants of uneven talent. This reflects an indifference to—even a contempt for—undergraduate instruction.

Education involves, ideally, an alternating rhythm of idolatry and subversion, the authority principle and insurgency. The lecturer ravishes his audience intellectually. But the student must have the opportunity for defiance and counterattack. And a graduate assistant, often little removed from a bright undergraduate, does not provide an appropriate object of attack. It is this question-asking, idol-smashing phase that is the key to real learning. The other, quiescence in the lecture hall, is often merely busy-work. A gifted teacher at Smith College (a school loaded with teaching talent) remarked wryly, "Any good student wants to burn down the place by the time she's a senior."

The stringencies of the next ten years may bring about a revolution with the happiest consequences for higher education. Independent study is the first of the new models, born of the need for economy and reinforced by a hangover of Deweyism. (It is Deweyan in that it is anchored in the individual interest of the student.) Its most attractive feature is that it sets up habits which endure long after college. What, after all, can college teachers hope to achieve during four painfully unsettled years in the life of a student? All that can be done is to set the stage hopefully for a lifetime of study. If a student develops the habit of reading with discrimination, he may be reasonably well educated by the time he is thirty. Independent study provides an impetus in this direction. At the least, the independent-study candidates learn their way around a library—a rare skill, I might add, among young and old.

Through independent study students may win back their identity which rote learning kills off. I had a sobering lesson in the stultification of students recently. I asked a literature class I was teaching to read a background book and do a critical commentary. Paper after paper proved to be little more than a summary. With some exasperation I asked why this happened when I had specifically asked for critical impressions.

"It was safer that way," students said. "It's what we thought you wanted; it's what other instructors usually want."

How casually they forswear their own identities!

If there is to be life-adjustment education—and we seem to be stuck with it all the way through college—let us at least have a sensible timetable. Let us teach the basic skills where they belong: in high school. And the colleges should do something currently done—prematurely and badly—in high school: consumer training, so to speak, in the arts. In high school there is the barbarism of the book report and the magazine "unit." (The word "unit," so modish in pedagogy, gives the game away with its phony intimation of precision.) High school kids dutifully plow through "good" books, riffle the pages of the *Atlantic* or *Harper's*, and make callow judgments about movies and plays. Yet in college, at precisely the time when students will inherit the world—and its arts—there is little concern with them. Isn't there something absurd about colleges vacating their responsibility to mold civilized taste? It is little wonder that so many college graduates are cultural infants reading best-selling pap.

Under the influence of a distorted progressivism, colleges have pushed into areas in which they don't belong. The brash imperialism of personnel services and student activities strives to dominate the students' private and social life. In contrast with today's organized fun, there was something innocent about the horseplay of the twenties. At least the hell-raisers were autonomous. Their infantilism wasn't sponsored by the administration, which these days lays down the ground rules and acts as umpire for the nursery games. There is even a dreadful sameness about campus activities from coast to coast, for the personnel technicians are quick to import wholesome nonsense from other campuses.

My quarrel with the personnel engineers is that they are likely to be smiling, smiling products of Teachers College or some other emporium of inane good will and well-roundedness. And all too frequently they are undereducated themselves. Yet they shape decisions which are academic ones, for every decision on a college campus is academic. And they fuss too much over students. I challenge the concern with student mental hygiene and the close supervision of student organizations—"psychiatric babysitting" someone called it. On examination, it often turns out to be something quite different: the will to power on the part of administrators. It is another instance of the invasion of privacy that characterizes our time.

Isn't there in all this nervous hovering over students a subtle denigration of any ideas they may have? And don't students become infected with excessive caution, with the disabling sense that their ideas are not really to be trusted? (In Queens College in New York, the two student newspapers were supplanted by a single one despite student protest. The action evoked a litany among students of the futility of their efforts.) There has to be another choice than monolithic squaredom or disheveled Bohemianism.

The effort to shape personality or inculcate manners through administrative machinery doesn't work. A student develops by knowing and admiring the educated man or woman who behaves with restraint and expressiveness. What the large academic mills need desperately is what the good, small, liberal arts colleges have built into them: the opportunity for contact between students and teachers, occasions for the exchange of ideas uncontaminated by notebook or grade.

The estate of the college professor has gone up; he is even an authority figure of sorts. But this only aggravates an old and vexing paradox. If his status is high, his income is still low—probably a few cuts lower, on the average, than that of a member of the Teamsters Union. The professor's characteristic bearing is one of dignified self-pity.

The image of the college teacher has become youthful. No longer viewed as a crotchety ancient with a bizarre passion for Middle High German phonology or pre-Columbian art, he has probably shed twenty years in the last few decades. He is now businesslike, brisk, and crew-cut—a cocktail party ornament. Nevertheless, shading into the new image is the old clerk of Oxford—prim, vaguely eunuchoid, and cloistered. People expect college professors to resist the infections of American life. (At the same time they expect them to be frantically up to date.)

Academics, while beginning to resemble businessmen, have all sorts of special burdens. Absurd standards of gentility prevail. (A faculty tea is truly a parody of itself: the stifling politesse, the elegant noncommunication, the shuffling for position.) But the main thing is that there is not enough money; life is pinched and mean (except for the new expense-account aristocracy who get the big grants). A dean of a college in the Northeast told me that a good deal of his time is spent writing character references to finance companies. Thus a promotion, let us say, to associate professor is likely to be a more desperate matter than a hitch up the corporate ladder. A $400-raise to a teacher with a second or third child on the way can be a necessity for survival.

As a result, academic institutions are not gentle, civilized re-treats, high, high above the dark jungle of business. Alas, at precisely the time that business has become somewhat less feral, academia now dances to the beat of the tom-tom. It has come to resemble the world outside when the world outside no longer resembles what it was. The competitiveness is exacerbated by the new marginal groups now in academic life. Universities were once dominated by Anglo-Saxon oligarchs, often with independ-ent incomes (the professor's favorite daydream). Today second- and third-generation immigrant groups of all nationalities, in America's new status revolution, have found their way into academic life, are pouring their energies into it, and threshing about for position. This makes for a much-needed vitality but also for sharp elbows and knees when the in-fighting gets rough.

But the big problem is the relationship of the scholarly routines to the intellectual life. To put it plainly, all too often universities are simply research factories with little relationship to that bold exercise of ideas which should be the peculiar genius of an institution of higher learning. Intellectualism and teaching do not pay off; research does, since it builds professional prestige— the key factor in the academic market place. (A marvelously funny sketch could be written about scholarly conventions in which no one listens to the papers being read. Instead, everybody mills around in the corridors and lobby converted into a shape-up or hiring hall, the chairmen looking for bright young men—and bright young men—looking for jobs.) The problem has become worse as knowledge has proliferated—the process of Balkanization run amuck. There are all these little fiefs of knowledge in this crabbed medievalism, in which one communicates incestuously only with his scholarly first cousins. Publish or perish, the deadly old choice, has become—publish *and* perish.

Scholarly caution can freeze the intellectual and imaginative faculties. The most uncommon kind of teaching, but the most important, is what might be called relational: seeing the connections between things, throwing bridges from one area of knowledge to another. A young assistant professor was describing the university where he received his Ph.D., "All that dull Germanic scholarship . . . if you had an opinion, watch out!" "The Groves of Ac-anemia," a sprightly Ph.D. candidate called her university, one of the great schools of the East. "All those bloodless people," she added shudderingly.

One answer is to infuse college faculties with new life. We have writers in residence. Why not visiting professorships—or lectureships—for talented businessmen, journalists, trade-union people? (The point is to break up the monopoly now operating in restraint of intellectual trade.) The outlanders might pick up some academic circumspection, while their daring and sense of the concrete might rub off on the scholastics. It might be a good idea to apply the Antioch scheme of education to academicians. (At Antioch students have a work period each year in which they have a chance to relate what they learn to the flinty realities outside.)

College faculties should be shaken up a little. Intramural warfare notwithstanding, life is too easy for many. There are the ineluctable corruptions of teaching: the too-quick dominion over students' minds, the sleazy omniscience, the sacerdotal aura of the lectern. It would be wise to have more faculty seminars, and teams of teachers handling the same class in active opposition to each other. All too often it is considered bad taste for professors to discuss ideas—they are inherently monologists—and some faculty dining rooms have the starchy chattiness of a British officers' mess.

The welfare state can be just as enervating in academic circles as elsewhere. And current tenure arrangements can mean strenuous effort early in one's career and the worst kind of sloth in the middle and final stages when one should be most productive.

But the problem of scholarship is more complex than I have indicated. On the one hand, universities and colleges should be more than conveyor belts. There is, no doubt, an organic connection between firsthand scholarship and teaching. There can be a special excitement for the student in contact with minds working on the frontiers of knowledge. On the other hand, there has to be a halt to the trivialization of scholarship, the rage to publish. "Who says that 10,000 political scientists have to publish?" a professor in California said impatiently. "How many scholars can dance on the head of an academic journal?" an observer asked. Certainly, the consequence of avid brigades of researchers trying to establish scholarly beachheads is the creation of new scholarly journals and university presses, which pour out a flood tide of the dull and repetitive—an expense of spirit in a waste of footnotes. This torrent of words threatens to engulf any reasonably conscientious reader. An English professor retorted testily, when I complained about the rash of new scholarly journals, "But they're not meant to be read. They're supposed to be indexed."

A distinction should be made between a scholarly cast of mind and actual scholarship. Every college teacher should be scholarly; it is a minimum obligation. But he need not publish to be scholarly. In fact, the publishing process drives him into academic dustbins and deflects him from broader scholarly concerns. (In almost every English department there is the man who says, "Faulkner? I don't know anything about him or care about him. He's out of my area.") We need fewer scholarly journals and greater intellectual commerce among disciplines, especially between the humanities and the sciences. And with this retrenchment, there should be a new emphasis on teaching—undergraduate teaching— with the best people reaching as many students as possible. Scholarship, yes, but without the fetishistic overtones it now has. It may also be that if the petty scholarly empires are reduced, good scholars may turn their minds to problems of higher education instead of letting the educationists win by default.

William James' attack on the "Ph.D. octopus" is still relevant. The narrow guild character of the academic profession with its emphasis on the Ph.D., means that talented teachers without the Ph.D. are consigned to a squalid *Lumpenproletariat*. (As our society becomes increasingly bureaucratized, credentials take on more and more importance. Consider the absurd role of the B.A. as the way to the abundant life.)

We ought seriously to consider whether there is any point in the whole Ph.D. process. In university circles the degree is irritably dismissed as a union card, and perhaps it is nothing more than that—an indefensible form of academic featherbedding. Certainly it would be hard to demonstrate that the Ph.D. is evidence either of teaching skill or of the ability to make an original contribution to knowledge. (Its disastrous effect on the native vigor of one's prose is notorious.) The most one can say for it is that it attests to a certain minimum of intelligence and plenty of *Sitzfleisch*. Veterans of the Ph.D. grind will affirm that preparation for the orals is little more than an ordeal of memorizing. (The information promptly leaks out of the candidate's mind after the exam.) And who, in his right mind, ever reads the run-of-the-mill Ph.D. dissertation?

College teachers should be recruited in terms of realistic criteria: the ability to think, skill in imparting knowledge and stimulating thought, and that ineffable quality of enthusiasm without which the classroom becomes a mortuary.

Guild parochialism means that some of the best people have the hardest time. Dennis Wrong wrote recently of the "humanistic underground" in American sociology, fighting a forlorn battle against an IBM-oriented and lifeless empiricism. The members of this underground have to endure names like "journalist" and "literature major." The International of the discipline is rigid and unforgiving.

A professor of sociology in the Midwest offered a modest and revealing rationale for the kind of piddling research that abounds. "You see," he explained, "it provides a function for the guys who are not so talented—you know, those with an IQ of 115 or 120. On their own, they can't do very much. But give them a little area to work in, and then put together what they have done and what others have done, and maybe you'll have something. Sure, there are people like Riesman with powerful minds, but what are you going to do with less gifted people?"

There is no time to discuss the jolly fratricide in which scholars pummel each other in academic journals. Nor can I more than mention the opaque prose, the esoteric cult-language through which scholars protect their spooky guild secrecy. Curiously enough, a scholar whose style is uncluttered and vigorous (in a word, unprofessorial) can probably place an article sooner in a reputable national magazine than in an academic journal, so intense is the rat race. Moreover, the material will appear faster, he will be paid, and the article will evoke response from a wide range of people. When one lucky pedant does place a scholarly article, he grows old waiting for it to appear, and the only reward is a handful of free copies. (In fact, it usually costs the scholar dear, since he is likely to order a few hundred offprints to distribute among his peers.) Of course, in many academic precincts publishing in a national magazine does not rate—again, the sterile scholasticism that gives university life such a scrawny look.

This specialized intellectual efficiency, unfortunately, is picked up by graduate students, a notably timid group. Because of the recent wealth of fellowships and grants, careerism gets off to an early start among graduate students, who are inclined anyway to be opportunists at best and sycophants at worst. Weren't we better off with the lonely young men reading their heads off without a cold eye cocked at a grant of $3,000 a year? There are few graduate schools without the pale copies of the Great Men. When the altar boys receive their Ph.D.'s, they are dispatched to the hinterland with the Word. A few years ago I took a seminar at Columbia with Lionel Trilling and was appalled at the shameless fashion with which the young graduate students echoed Mr. Trilling's ideas. In all fairness, Trilling did not himself encourage this iconolatry. On occasion, he would deliberately shake up his students by taking new and unexpected intellectual tacks. But how many Trillings are there? Elsewhere, there must be masters who relish their role.

It is well to remember that the graduate student, often subsidized by the university, desperately needs his department's recommendation. This, more than anything else, will determine where he is placed, and his initial placement may well set the tone of his career. Graduate professors, on the other hand, have the assurance of a captive and submissive audience. How good do they have to be? (The effectiveness of teaching varies inversely with the level. High school teachers are usually more skillful as teachers—not as scholars—than college teachers. Undergraduate instruction tends to be better than graduate teaching.)

The effect of all this is narrowness, intellectual pallor, professionalization—the very antitheses of the goals of liberal education. C. Wright Mills made this bitter estimate of the younger social scientists:

> I have seldom seen one of these young men in a condition of genuine intellectual puzzlement. And I have never seen any passionate curiosity about a great problem, the sort of curiosity that compels the mind to travel anywhere and by any means, to remake itself if necessary, in order to find out. These young men are less restless than methodical; less imaginative than patient. . . . Listening to their conversations, trying to gauge the quality of their curiosity, one finds a deadly limitation of mind.

A word about faculty democracy, another sacred cow. Committees have been growing like a cancer in most colleges as the vehicle of faculty self-determination. On the surface, the trend is unobjectionable—who is against democracy?—but committees can be a curse. For one thing, teaching is a demanding art; one wonders about the wisdom of dispersing the teacher's energies. Secondly, committees and policy-making lead to a complicated network of relationships and an enforced, often neurotic, intimacy. In the old days, you hated your chairman, or the president —or both. Now you hate everybody.

Since I am now comfortably installed at New York University, an urban institution with a healthy intellectual and emotional climate, I am somewhat insulated against the Gothic excesses of the academic world. But I am constantly aghast at the rocketing anxieties of academic friends who teach all around the country. Serving on a tenure committee is exceeded in melodramatic horror only by being a candidate for tenure. "You don't understand what we go through," a friend at a savagely competitive but highly ingrown university told me. "You would have to be here all the time."

I have proposed some tentative answers to real dilemmas in higher education. But practical answers must flow from a vision of what the educated man should be. More than ever, we have to be concerned with first principles. We cannot teach everything —or everyone. What do we really want from our colleges? That education should emerge as high drama in our popular press is at least a symptom of health.

There are even signs that the current generation of students is rousing itself from its beauty sleep. Honor students at the University of Wisconsin petitioned recently for more strenuous challenges. At Smith College student sentiment seems overwhelmingly in favor of independent study starting in the freshman year. A Harvard student council report lashed out at the idea that a "non-committed, objective stance is the only one that is scholarly and scientific." And the lunchroom sit-in movement in the South, with its Northern support, is rousing proof that we may be entering a new era of energetic but judicious student activity. We may yet see that "wholly awakened man" for whom Woodrow Wilson called.

Higher education is a creature of our society, but it cannot escape its obligation to transcend it. We live in a dangerously easeful time. There is a lack of roughage in our national diet. Should not our colleges and universities provide a countervailing tendency to the fat, sleek materialism of American life? Shouldn't they provide something hard and lean and spiritually purposeful? The press of students at our college gates may give us just the opportunity we need. In the past, our fear of the idea of the superior few pushed us into shoddiness and hypocrisy. We are now in position to try the leap for excellence. We have the students; we even have the teachers. All we need is the will.

INDEX

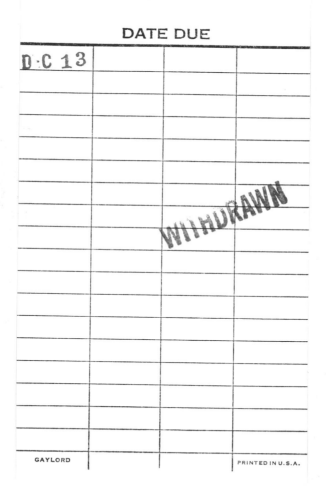